Fish Be With You
The Children's Guide to Aquarium Care

Written by

Fiel John Meria

 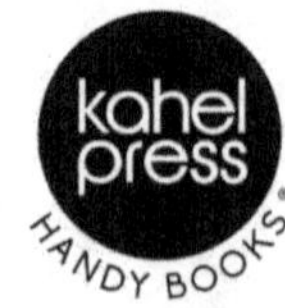

Fish Be With You: The Children's Guide to Aquarium Care

Text copyright © 2018 Fiel John Meria

Published in 2018 by St. Matthew's Publishing Corporation (through its imprint Kahel Press)
Publishers since 1989, with nationwide operations in the Philippines
for the distribution of educational books and children's books.

ISBN: 978-971-625-399-3

How to Order
Purchase individual copies from www.stmatthews.ph

Copies are also available at special rates in bulk orders. Contact the publisher through the details below.

St. Matthew's Publishing Corporation
First RVC Building, 92 Anonas Cor. K-6th Streets, East Kamias, Quezon City
(02) 8426-5611 || inquiry@stmatthews.ph
www.stmatthews.ph

This book is dedicated to two of my students who share
the same love in petkeeping as I do, Mio & Gian.

And to Pepper, my pet Hedgehog, whom I adopted and lived
a full life with my family and even graced my wedding.
He passed away on the day I finished this book.
You will be missed.

TABLE OF CONTENTS

So, Why an Aquarium?

A Word on Conservation

Siamese Fighting Fish & Dwarf Gourami • Guppies, & Swordtails • Neon & Cardinal Tetras • Corydoras • Zebra Danio

Goldfish - Oranda, Ryukin, & Ranchu • Medium Cichlids - Green Terror, Convict & Blood-red Jewel • Medium Bottom Dwellers - Plecostomus & Clown Loach • Medium Gourami - Pearl & Kissing Gourami • Round Cichlids - Freshwater Angelfish & Discus • Black Ghost Knife Fish

So, Why an Aquarium?

Hello! My name is John. As you can probably tell, I love aquarium fish. I've taken care of all sorts of animals, too—from dogs, hedgehogs, rabbits, sugar gliders and, at one point, I even worked at the zoo. But more than any other type of pet, I LOVE aquarium fish. Back in high school, many of my classmates even made fun of me because I loved aquarium fish so much. But, I didn't care! I love this hobby and I'm proud of it.

Most people think that taking care of aquarium fish is hard, but that isn't true at all. Any pet will have challenges, but compared to other animals, keeping aquarium fish is actually one of the easiest. All you need to do is just stick to the right aquarium size you can maintain, and do the right routines, most of which require little time and effort.

I remember that, before I got my first aquarium, I brought a pet goldfish home from the wet market. I coaxed my mom to buy me a goldfish, and she said yes. The seller just gave me the goldfish in a small plastic bag, together with a smaller packet of fish food pellets. I was told to just "keep it in a container." I did as the seller told me. Sadly, after just a few days, the goldfish died and I felt sad. The worst part of it was that the seller made money knowing fully well that the fish would hopelessly die in the condition he recommended.

After that, I learned the basics of aquarium keeping. I was determined never to let that happen again. I bought many books and studied them closely. I went to pet stores often and interviewed the owners and the maintenance crew. I even visited many aquarium experts in my home country and learned a lot from them.

After learning from all these experiences, I summarized them here into 7 easy-to-understand steps. Note that these steps are more of "principles" and not "rules." Learning principles is better than learning rules because this means that, if you get how to do something, you will eventually develop your own style. Through this book, it is my hope that you'll develop your own style as an aquarist and have as much joy as I've had in this hobby.

Like any other kind of petkeeping, becoming an aquarist has its own benefits. You get to learn discipline, responsibility and value for life. You also learn more about biology and about the animals you take care of. Lastly, you develop a bond with your pet and have a special connection with them.

There are also certain things that you only get to achieve with an aquarium and not with other pets. This includes creating your own ecosystem—a whole world filled with life in the corner of your living room. It means that an aquarium doubles as a piece of decoration as well. You also do not need to spend a lot of time with your fish nor do you contend with strong smells associated with them.

Basic Set up

Usually, any beginning aquarist would want to start with a small aquarium set-up. And with this, you can already put a few small fish inside. Just to get things started, the following set-up contains basic equipment and small fish that is inexpensive and quite easy to maintain.

- 5 pieces of Fantail Guppies
- 5.0 Gallon Aquarium
- Aquarium Air Pump
- Aquarium Air Hose
- Undergravel Filter
- Aquarium Gravel
- Flake Fish Food
- Anti-chlorine Solution

As you advance in knowledge, you can take care of medium- and large-sized fish. In this category, you'll find some fish such as the discus, the flowerhorn, and the arowana that are happy to see their owners and forge a bond with them just like with dogs and cats. In many cases, they even allow themselves to be stroked when their owner puts their hand into the aquarium.

For those looking for a challenge, the marine aquarium is a worthy set-up. Some examples of fish you can keep in a marine aquarium are clownfish, sea anemones, eels, rays and even sharks. When you have one of these, it's like having an ocean park at home!

TRIVIA! All forms of life we have discovered have scientific names and that includes fish! Most of these names will seem weird and hard to pronounce like *Apteronotus albifrons*. That's because scientific names are in the Latin language so that scientists from different countries have just one name for every species.

Everything you need to learn about keeping your own aquarium, from beginner to expert levels, is found in this little book. It's proudly complete and made as simple to understand as possible. Follow the directions carefully and, hopefully, you'll be one of the many people in the world who enjoy this amazing and satisfying hobby.

A Word on Conservation

Aquarium keeping brings people joy and it should be kept that way for many years to come. Sadly, however, the reality is that since so many people want to make more money selling aquarium fish, they turn greedy and do bad things.

To prevent this, one needs to practice good conservation as an aquarist. Conservation can mean many things, but in the aquarium hobby it means making sure that those who breed, sell and buy fish go about it in a way that doesn't harm the environment or the quality of the fish.

The good thing is that it's easy to spot bad seller practices. So to help, don't buy from pet stores where you see the following:

X While it's normal to overcrowd certain fish tanks for selling, there are fish in pet stores that are TOO overcrowded. This affects the health of the fish and increases the chances of getting them sick.

X Fish in the pet stores look like they are in dirty, murky looking water. Pet stores should at least change part of the water in their tanks daily.

X Fish that are obviously sick or worse, dead, but then the seller does not quarantine or remove them immediately. (To check what quarantine means, see page 36.)

X Illegally sold fish like the Red-bellied piranha (Pygocentrus nattereri) can easily be invasive species and ruin our rivers if someone were to ever dump them there.

X Sellers that will just convince you to buy more fish and overcrowd your own aquarium. (To find out how many fish you can fit, see page 11.)

X Sellers that sell aquatic animals that require special care, such as needing colder or warmer water but then they don't tell you. (See page 99 for some examples)

X Sellers that sell fish that have been colored with dye or have their tails clipped to make them shaped like hearts.

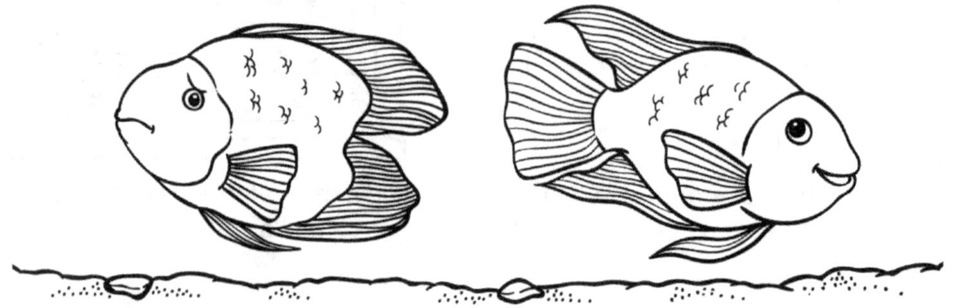

By not supporting these bad sellers and only supporting the good ones, you help out in making the hobby better and more popular for everyone. You'll also be more likely each fish in this book is labelled with their respective maximum sizes.

PART 1
7 Steps to Becoming a Good Aquarist

7 Steps to Becoming a Good Aquarist

An aquarist is a person who keeps an aquarium. When you get your own pet fish, you'll be considered an aquarist, too! However, not everyone who brings a fish home does it properly and it ends up in sad consequences, like the story in the beginning of the book. Thus, read these steps carefully before buying and bringing home your first aquarium.

STEP #1
Choose the Right Size of Aquarium and Number of Fish

Choosing the size of your aquarium is probably the single most important decision you'll need to make as an aquarist. Size determines so many things, including:

1. How easy it will be to clean and maintain the aquarium
2. What kinds of fish you can keep and how big they can grow
3. Where to put the aquarium

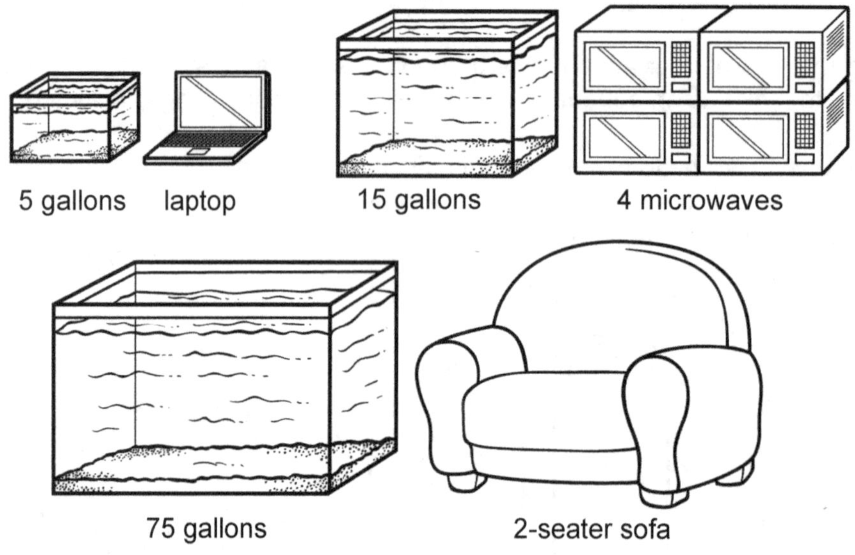

It is highly recommended to choose your first aquarium in between the 2.5-gallon to the 10-gallon range. Once you gain some experience in this small aquarium range, you can move into the 15- to 45-gallon range. For larger fish and saltwater aquaria, you need to get an aquarium range of at least 50 gallons.

In this book, fish are organized in a manner that rates their difficulty in terms of the size of the aquarium. This means that beginner fish are the small ones (less than 1 inch to about 4 inches), intermediate would be medium-sized fish (5 to 12 inches) and expert would be above 12 inches as well as the saltwater aquarium, since saltwater aquaria will need to be big anyway.

Number of Fish in Your Aquarium

The size of your aquarium determines the number and the size of the fish you can fit in it. This is important because an aquarium that is too small for the fish or has too many fish (this is called "overstocking") will lead to your fish getting stressed, sick, and have a much shorter lifespan. In general, it's better to keep an aquarium that is too big for your fish rather than too small for them.

Aquarists have a long discussion on how much fish they can keep and what size can be kept. While this discussion can get complicated, experience shows that following this simple rule keeps things safe:

1 INCH OF FISH FOR EVERY 1 GALLON IN THE AQUARIUM

You'll know the fish's standard length by measuring from the tip of its mouth until the caudal peduncle, as illustrated below.

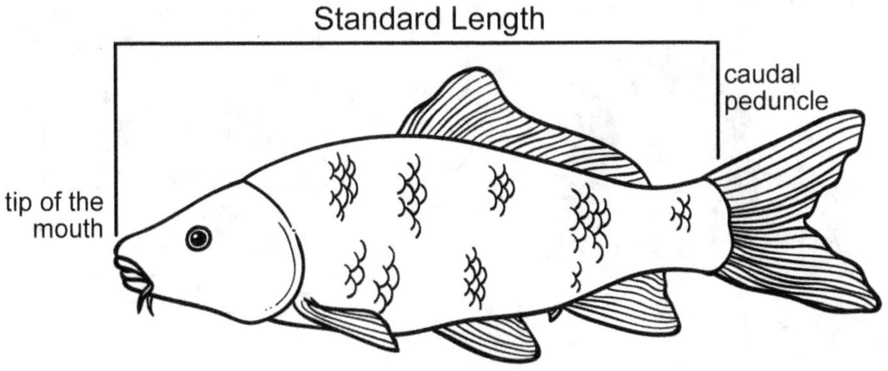

A VERY IMPORTANT thing to keep in mind: the aquarium you get should NOT be dependent on the size when you get the fish, but on the maximum size of that fish. To know the maximum size of the fish from mouth to caudal peduncle, each fish in this guide will have this description.

For example, a 2.5-gallon aquarium can accommodate about 2.5 inches of fish. By this principle, you can fit about five male fantail guppies in a 2.5-gallon aquarium (male guppies tend to be smaller than female fantail guppies, they grow to about half an inch or 0.5 inches from the mouth to the caudal peduncle).

The thing is, most fantail guppies are sold very close to their maximum size. However, most fishes are not sold at their maximum size, but are sold much smaller than that. For example, Convict Cichlids (*Amatitlania nigrofasciata*) are typically sold as less than 1-inch fish, but they can grow up to 4 to 6 inches! Thus, you shouldn't fit two small Convict Cichlids in a 2.5-gallon aquarium. Instead, you'd be better off placing two of them in a 10-gallon aquarium.

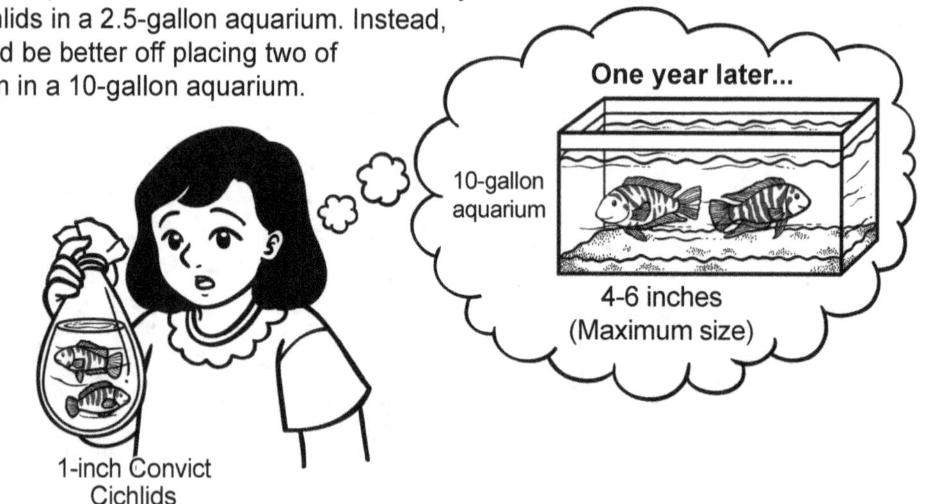

What if I Overload my Aquarium?

To be perfectly honest, most aquarists tend to overload their aquaria a little just to squeeze a few more fish. It is possible to overload on the "1 inch per 1 gallon" rule since as mentioned, it's just a general guideline and not a hard rule. This means that there are certain recommendations to keep in mind before you overload:

1. Do not go beyond the maximum ratio of 1.5 inches to 1 gallon.
2. At any point, if your tank is always dirty, your fish are not growing or you find that they tend to fight, do not add any more fish.
3. Add one more partial water change to your week to help keep the aquarium cleaner for your fish. (On water changes, see 42).

4. If your aquarium is still full of growing fish, do not overload. Adding more fish will stunt their growth, stress them more and lower their lifespan. In other words, it's better to overload with fully-grown fish.
5. In relation to #4, if your current fish are already fully grown but you wish to add a growing fish, do not overload.
6. If your aquarium is not the typical shape and is more prolonged or heightened for decorative purposes, do not overload.

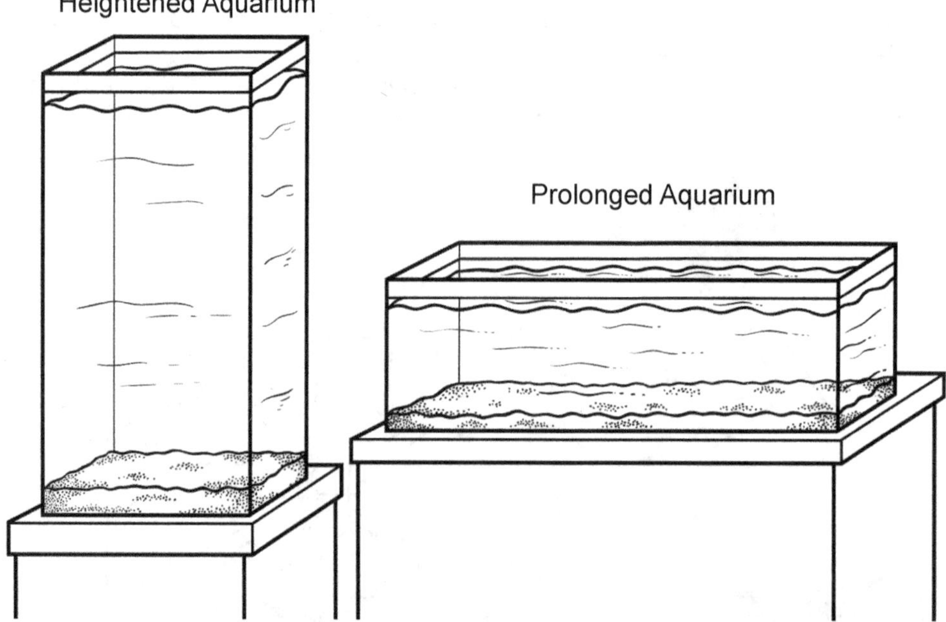

Once you have determined the right size of aquarium as well as the size and number of fish you can keep, the next step is learning other types of equipment used for aquaria.

Step #2
Learn Basic Materials and Equipment Used for Aquaria

Now that you know the right size and amount of fish to put in it, it's time to discuss equipment that are used to maintain an aquarium.

Essential Materials and Equipment

These are equipment that you buy alongside the aquarium and are definitely needed if you want to bring home and set up your aquarium properly.

Filtration System - This is the single most important equipment you'll buy aside from the aquarium itself. It enables the fish to breathe and helps keep the water clean as well. (Read more about filtration systems on page 21.)

Fish Food - There are many different types of fish food since different fish have different dietary requirements. (Read more about feeding and maintaining your fish properly on page 37.)

Anti-chlorine Solution - This is a clear liquid that removes chlorine from your tap water. Chlorine is a substance used to clean water and can be fatal to your fish. To use the Anti-chlorine Solution, simply put in the recommended amount in your water. Wait for about 30 minutes before your water can already accommodate fish. If your tap has a built-in filter that already removes chlorine, this solution won't be needed.

Plastic or Styrofoam Cooler - It is highly advisable to have a cooler ready to store the plastic bags from when your fish are transported home. This helps minimize the stress on the fish on the drive going home as leaving them in a plastic bag inside the car can cause the fish to be rocked about and be exposed to the heat or cold.

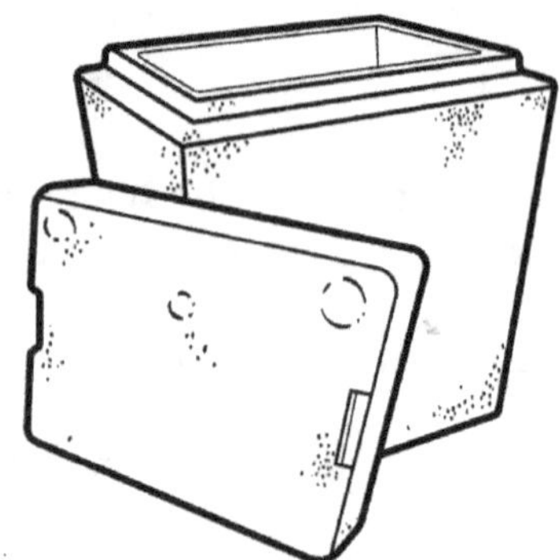

Fish Net - It is necessary if you plan to transfer to other fish tanks or even do a general cleaning of an aquarium. Buy a fish net that is appropriate for the size of your fish and your tank. Using your hands or other containers not meant for catching fish inside your aquarium can bruise or hurt your fish. When using this, net your fish gently, one at a time and transfer it quickly. Minimize their time inside the net. Make sure they are not out of the water and inside the net for more than 5 seconds. The less time in the net, the better because their fins can get damaged when they struggle.

Aquarium Salt - Buy this from your aquarium store. Keep a bag stashed away since it is used to cure a number of fish illnesses for freshwater fish such as the dreaded anchor worm and fish lice. Unlike other types of fish medication, this doesn't spoil easily and can be stored away for years. While regular salt can be bought from the supermarket, there's no guarantee that these do not contain harmful ingredients that would harm your aquarium fish.

Aquarium Stand - This is typically a strong, stainless steel stand that can hold the weight of an aquarium. Other kinds of stands are made of less durable material such as wood or plastic that can even double as cabinets to house other aquarium equipment. Make sure that the material used for your aquarium stand is able to take on the weight of your aquarium. Buy from reputable sellers and avoid "custom making" your own unless the manufacturer has a track record of making aquarium stands. An aquarium of 10 gallons weighs a little over 100 pounds! Thus, never underestimate the weight of an aquarium.

<u>Situational Materials and Equipment</u>

These equipment are great to have but are only needed depending on the situation.

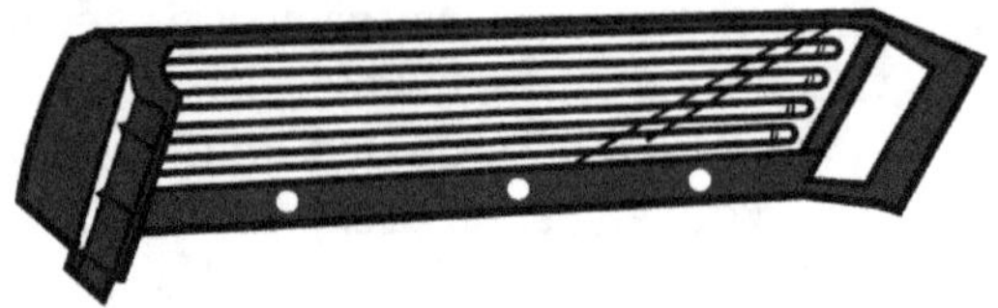

Lighting Fixture - Lighting is highly recommended if you want to observe your fish at their most beautiful. A light rod should last about two (2) years or more. Generally, you turn this on only when you are displaying your fish. Certain types of light are needed to maintain certain aquatic plants. The correct size of lighting fixture for your aquarium should cover the entire length of your tank.

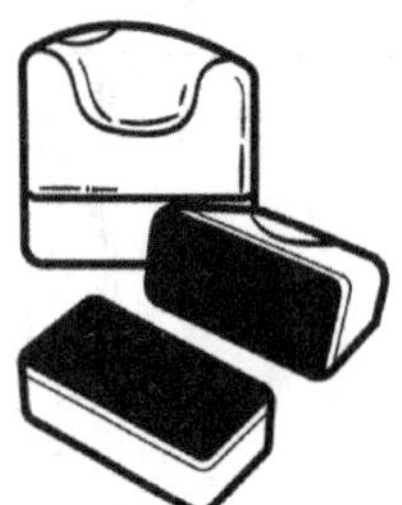

Magnetic Aquarium Cleaner - This allows you to clean algae from the inside of the aquarium glass. It's basically two magnetic pads that are stuck to one another through the glass, with the inside pad having a cleaning sponge as a surface. This is suitable for larger tanks but is usually unnecessary for smaller tanks as a simple sponge (that hasn't been exposed to soap) would suffice.

Aquarium Vacuum Hose - While a regular garden hose cut a bit shorter would do, an aquarium vacuum hose is still best. It is basically a regular hose with a cylindrical mouth. By filling this up with water and then putting the mouth near the gravel and pointing the other end to a bucket, you drain your aquarium for water changes while cleaning any uneaten food and fish feces from the gravel or floor of the aquarium.

Heater, Chiller and Thermometer - These three equipment combine to make sure that you control your aquarium's temperature in the right levels since different fishes you can keep require different temperatures. In tropical countries, the vast majority of owners will not need these since the majority of fish on the market are tropical fish. However, in colder countries and in rooms that are always airconditioned, a heater may be necessary.

Battery-Operated Aquarium Pump with Air Hose and Airstone - This can be used if you expect to have power outages in your area. While a few hours won't kill your fish, extended time in which the filtration system isn't working will be fatal to them especially if your aquarium is overloaded. In the event of a power outage, simply insert the batteries inside, plug the aquarium air hose to the battery-operated aquarium pump then put the airstone on the other side. Place the battery pump in a secure location on top of the aquarium, dip the airstone in and turn it on. You'll know it's working properly when you see fine bubbles coming out of the airstone.

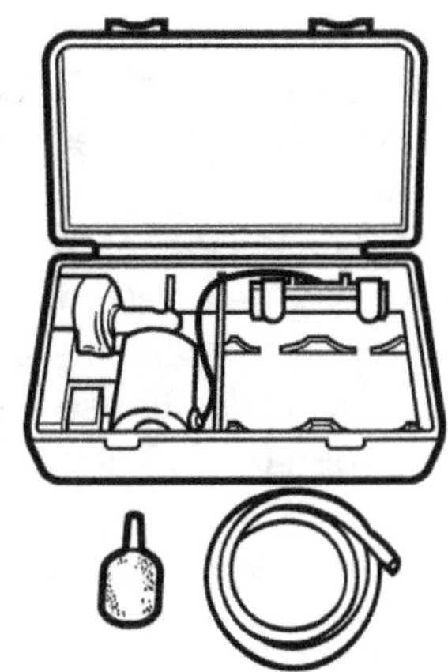

Fish Illness Medications - This ranges from general medication to medication specific to certain fish illnesses as well as methylene blue — a dark blue substance that prevents the growth of fungi. It is not recommended to get them when you first get an aquarium. Over time, these medications lose their potency, which is their ability to help sick fish become well. The best thing to do is to buy them as you need them.

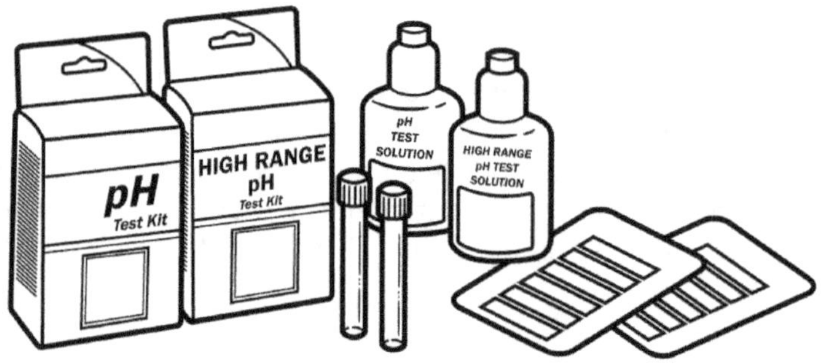

pH and Ammonia Testers - pH determines how alkaline or acidic the water is while ammonia determines the amount of unprocessed harmful fish waste that is dissolved in the water. When an aquarium is kept clean through weekly water changes, in most cases these won't be important for freshwater aquaria except for certain types of fish. They become very important though for saltwater aquaria where the fish and other organisms are more sensitive to changes in pH and ammonia levels. If you ever wish to use a pH tester, a good range to have in a freshwater aquarium is between 6.5-7.5 and an 8.0 for a saltwater aquarium.

As for specific equipment for saltwater aquaria, they will be covered in the marine portion of this book on the expert chapter on page 90.

STEP #3
Set Up a Fish Tank and an Adequate Filtration System

In the "So, Why an Aquarium?" portion of the book, a story was told about a goldfish dying when just kept in any container. So, why did it die?

Answer: It couldn't breathe.

Just like how it's hard to breathe when a room is too crowded or cramped, that goldfish couldn't breathe because the oxygen in the water he was in ran out.

To make sure that there's oxygen in the water, the most basic thing to do is set up a filtration system. This ensures that oxygen-rich air from the outside mixes frequently with the water in the aquarium, as well as help to clean it.

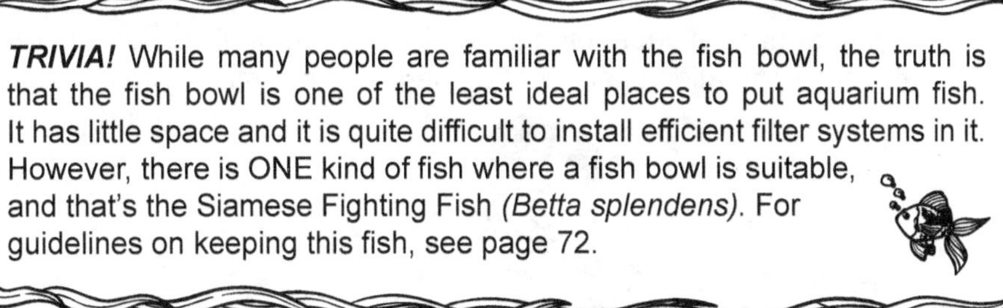

TRIVIA! While many people are familiar with the fish bowl, the truth is that the fish bowl is one of the least ideal places to put aquarium fish. It has little space and it is quite difficult to install efficient filter systems in it. However, there is ONE kind of fish where a fish bowl is suitable, and that's the Siamese Fighting Fish *(Betta splendens)*. For guidelines on keeping this fish, see page 72.

Before you can set up a filtration system, you need to prepare your tank. The steps are the following:

1. Wash your aquarium with tap water without using any type of detergent or soap.
2. Put water inside halfway and wipe the sides with a towel.
3. Carefully turn your aquarium sideways and displace the water.
4. Place the aquarium on the stand and move the entire assembly, including the stand to where you want it to be.
5. Make sure it is near a plug or an extension cord for your filtration system and light fixture.
6. Avoid places that are exposed to direct sunlight since this can drastically change the water's temperature and make too much algae grow in your tank.
7. Fill it up with water and check to see if any water is leaking. If there are any leaks, bring it back to the aquarium store for replacement or repairs.
8. Drain the aquarium afterwards by using your aquarium vacuum hose.

You will set up your aquarium depending on the type of filter that you have. There are many different types of filtration systems, but there are four main types.

Type #1 - The Undergravel Filter

An undergravel filter is fit at the bottom-most part of the aquarium, and then covered with aquarium gravel (pebbles). This is the perfect type of filter for beginners who want to start a small aquarium, from about 2.5 to 10 gallons in size.

To set it up, simply do the following:

1. Place your aquarium and its stand in an ideal place and put the undergravel filter in it. Make sure the aquarium is in the right spot before putting the gravel inside, or else it will be too heavy to move.

2. Get some gravel that is enough to fill your aquarium at least one inch above your filter base. Place the gravel inside a bucket. DON'T put the gravel in the aquarium yet.

3. While the gravel is inside the bucket, rinse it with water several times. This is done by filling the bucket with the gravel in it with water, then using
your hand to swirl it around, then emptying the bucket of water.
Do this three (3) times.

4. Carefully and slowly pour the gravel inside the aquarium.

5. Place a normal dish plate in the middle of the tank.

6. Connect a water hose to your faucet and pour on to the plate until your tank is filled but not overflowing. This will prevent the water from becoming murky. If your water is a little murky at this point, don't worry!

7. Connect the aquarium air pump to one end of the aquarium air hose and then the other end to the top of the underground filter. Plug in your air pump, and you'll know you did it right when there is a steady stream of bubbles going through the big portion of the filter.

8. Wait for a few hours or so and your aquarium will be magically clear!

To maintain an undergravel filter, simply drain the aquarium of water about once every six (6) months and run the gravel through the bucket again. Put about ¾ of your aquarium water back and replace the remaining ¼ with new water treated with antichlorine solution. Then just perform all the other steps as indicated here.

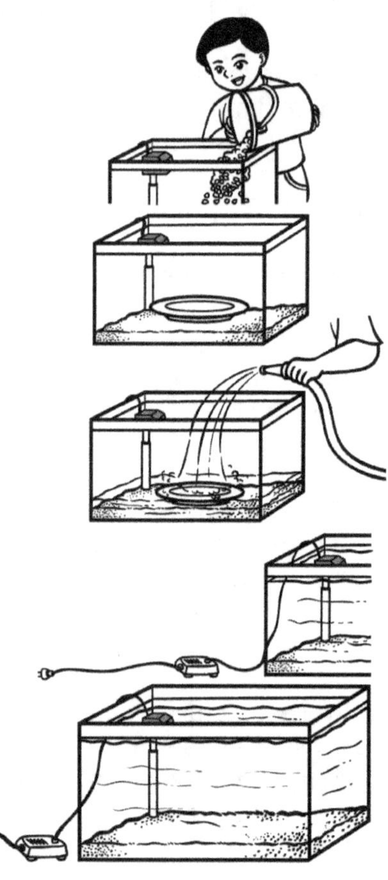

<u>**Type #2 - Foam and Corner Filters**</u>

Foam and corner filters work just like undergravel filters because they use an aquarium air pump. This means that they are good for small tanks from 2.5 to 10 gallons as well. However, they do require you to clean the foam about once a week, and then change it about once every two to three months. While it doesn't cost a lot, it is harder to maintain this type of filter. The advantage is that you can use this if you want to have a clear, plain aquarium since it does not require the gravel used in undergravel filters.

To set it up, simply do the following:

1. Place the aquarium where it needs to be and then fill it with water.

2. Place the filter in one lower corner of the aquarium and stick the suction cups in place.

3. Connect the aquarium air hose pump to the narrow end and the other in your aquarium air pump.

4. Plug the air pump.

5. You'll know you did it right when bubbles come out steadily through the wide end.

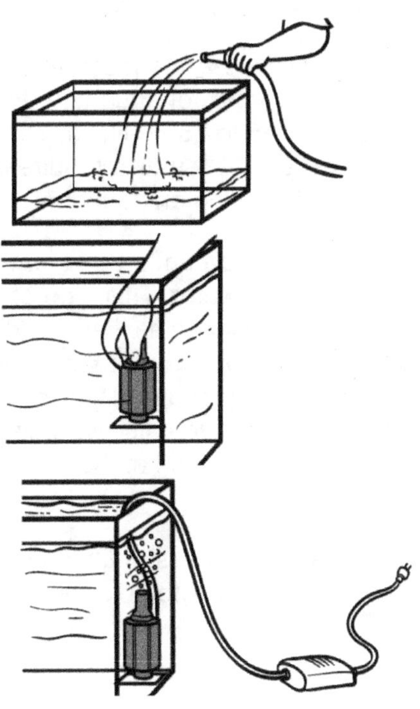

To maintain this filter, take out one of the foam filters once a month, wash the foam part, squeeze as hard as you can to get rid of the tap water, and then place it back. If you have more than one foam layered, just wash one at a time to maintain the healthy bacteria found in the other foam. DO NOT use soap as it can be harmful to your fish. The objective here is to simply get rid of the dirt stuck in the middle of the foam to make it effective in catching dirt once again. Once every three months, buy a replacement foam from your local aquarium store.

Type #3 - Overhead Filters

Overhead filters are the most versatile type of aquarium filter. There are overhead filters for every size of aquarium, though they are mostly used for medium to large aquaria from 15 to 150 gallons. They can be used for smaller aquaria, but they are more expensive. They also require a bit more maintenance but they generally do a better job at keeping an aquarium clean.

Instead of using a gentle aquarium air pump, they use a submersible water pump which circulates water. This type of system is not recommended for very small fish like guppies and tetras as they could get sucked in the water pump. You also need to make sure that you are using the right size of pump for your aquarium. If the pump is too small, your aquarium will not be cleaned properly. If it is too big, the water current will be too fast and your fish will be stressed, unhappy and may even die. To be sure, always look at the label of the water pump and make sure it is the right size for the aquarium you have.

You also use 2-3 layers of filter media. You normally want foam on top, followed by porous ceramic rings to help with biological filtration.

To set it up, simply do the following:

1. Insert the foam and other filter media (e.g. porous ceramic rings) with the foam always being the top layer.

2. When there are three or more layers, make sure the top layer contains the foam with the biggest holes, the next one with the smaller holes and the biological filter media at the bottom.

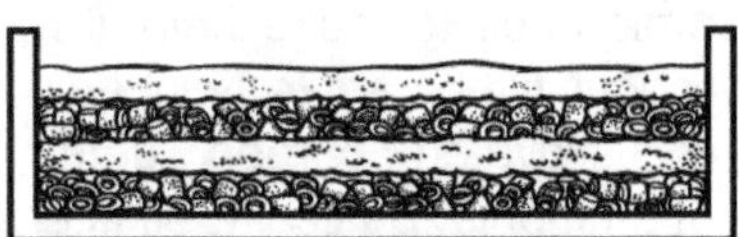

3. Place the overhead filter on top of your aquarium. Normally, you just place it on top of the aquarium glass or it's clipped on the side.

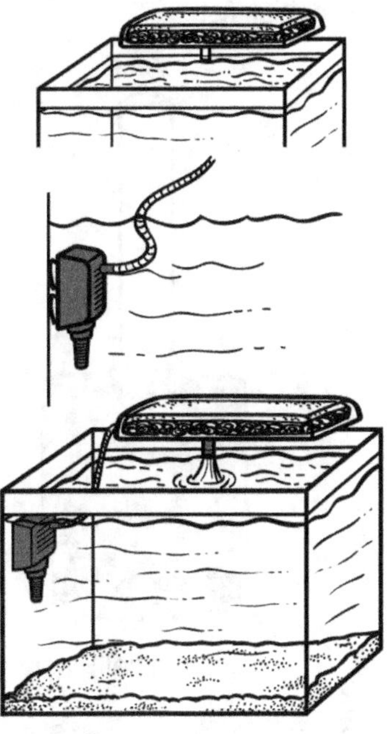

4. Submerge the water pump in the aquarium and stick it via its suction cups where the provided flexible hose can reach from the overhead filter.

5. Connect the flexible hose from the overhead filter on one end and the water pump on the other.

6. You'll know you did it right when there is a flow of water from your water pump, going through the filter media and back into your aquarium.

TRIVIA! There are actually three ways to filter the water in an aquarium: mechanical, biological and chemical. Mechanical filtration is when things that are large and visible to the naked eye are filtered from the water such as fish poop, uneaten food and dust. Biological filters are when you use porous surfaces, such as porous ceramic rings to make helpful bacteria which helps make the water of better quality. Chemical filters are advanced and usually used only in certain situations such as when activated carbon gets rid of poisons in the water and zeolite gets rid of ammonia. Basically, all filters have a bit of the first two and the third type is used in advanced situations, such as in marine (saltwater) aquariums or keeping very sensitive species or sick fish.

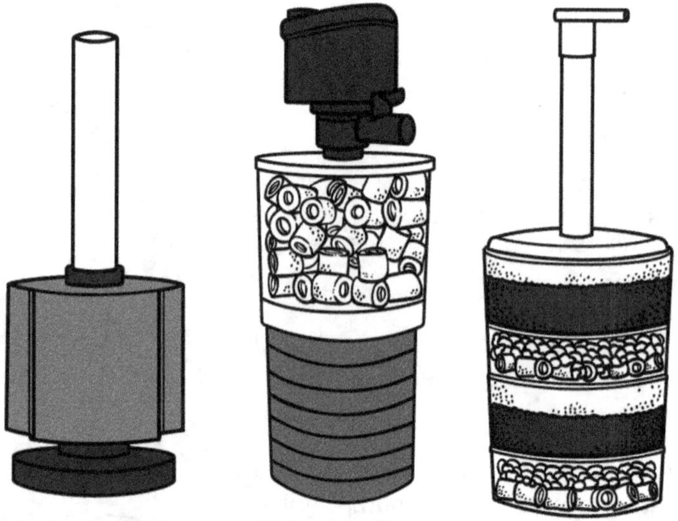

Mechanical Filter   Biological Filter   Chemical Filter

<u>**Type #4 - Canister filters**</u>

Canister filters are the most advanced form of filtration. They are usually used for very big tanks—anywhere in the 300 gallons to even in the tens and thousands of gallons!

Since they are also considered the best type of filter that help keep the aquarium clean, they are used by expert aquarists to keep marine aquarium fish and other very sensitive species.

Like the overhead filters, they use a motor to facilitate the movement of water and have layers of filter material inside the canisters. Often, canister filters are many times more expensive than other types of filters.

Every canister filter is a little different, and thus the set up is dependent on the instructions that you will find in its box.

Also, for marine aquaria, the canister filter is often times also used with other types of specialized filtration equipment. (Go to page 90 for setting up the marine aquarium).

If you did everything correctly, your aquarium set-up should look something like this:

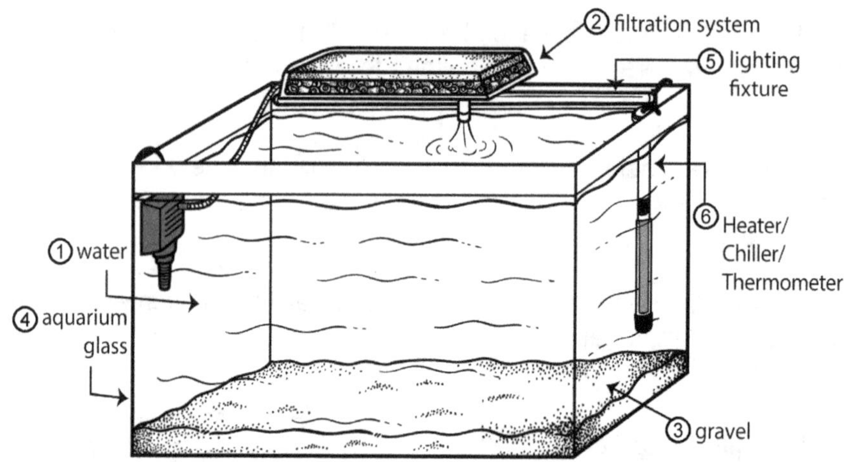

1. Water - slightly foggy is normal, and will be clear in just a few hours.
2. Filtration System - plugged in, water bubbling steadily for undergravel and foam filters, while it is running smoothly for overhead and canister filters. For overhead filters, the media are placed in the right order— foam on top and others below it.
3. Gravel - leveled and, if using an undergravel filter, completely covers it.
4. Aquarium Glass - no cracks, no leaks.
5. Lighting Fixture - install after everything is done; don't turn it on until the fish have already acclimated.
6. Heater / Chiller & Thermometer - only if needed.

Add some anti-chlorine solution to the water as per instructions on the bottle. Note that if you have activated charcoal as a filter medium, remove it first as it could interfere with the function of your anti-chlorine solution.

STEP #4
Pick Healthy Fish and Acclimate Them Properly

You're now ready to pick your fish! For most fish, Steps 1 to 4 can all be done on the same day. You can buy your aquarium and all the equipment you'll need including the fish and have it set up at home within a 1- to 2-hour period.

Picking healthy fish is not hard. However, there is also no such thing as a guarantee. Often times, you will encounter healthy looking fish but then they would become sickly during their first few days at home. If and when this happens, go read Step #6 on dealing with sick fish on page 43. Also, do not pick fish that are sick. Fish that are already sick have symptoms that are quite easy to see such as white spots, lifted scales and heavy breathing which you can also learn about in Step #6.

In addition, there are some other things you can look for to prevent bringing home sick fish that can be found in the quality of a pet store and the fish themselves.

Things to Look for in a Pet Store:
- Clear water in the tanks - This is due to water changes made by the staff.
- No dead or sick fish swimming around.
- A quarantine tank (To know what a quarantine tank is, read on in this chapter to page 36.)

Other Things to Look for When Picking Fish
- Responsiveness - When you put your hand above the tank, they react to your hand by either following your hand — expecting to be fed— or darting away immediately— thinking you're danger. Beware of fish that don't react at all.
- Physical Appearance - They have bright, excellent coloration and they don't have missing or torn fins, eyes or scales. When they have damage, it could indicate stress on the part of the fish, and stressed fish get sick more easily.

<u>**Transporting the Fish Home**</u>

Note that the first few days of your fish are the most critical for them. It is important that you minimize the stress on your fish as much as possible during this period of time. Even healthy fish, if exposed to a lot of stress, can have lowered immune systems that can cause them to get sick.

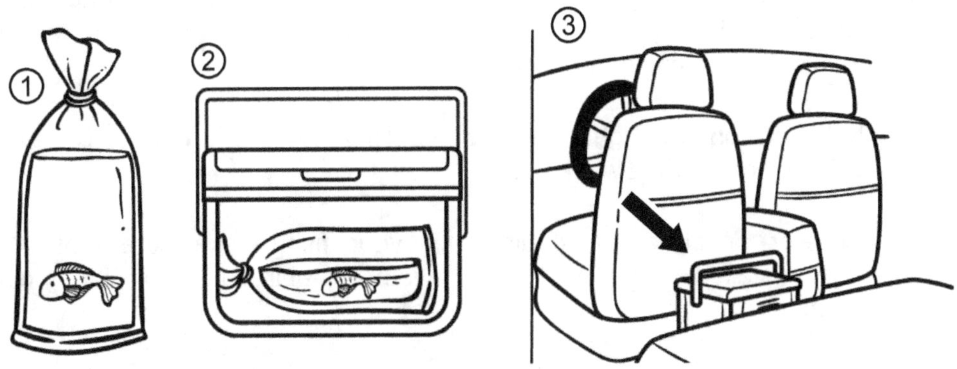

1. When you first buy your fish, they will usually be packaged in rubber band-sealed plastic bags filled with water and compressed air or oxygen.
2. Place the bags of fish in a plastic or styrofoam cooler. Close the lid to provide a more comfortable dark environment for your fish.
3. Place the cooler in a secure location in your car where it won't be rocked about as much.

Many stores that sell aquarium fish will tell you that you have a few hours to transport your fish, but it's actually best to minimize the time as much as possible. If you can get them from the pet store to your home in under 30 minutes, that would be best for your fish.

Putting Your First Fish in the Tank

Putting your first fish in the tank is a sensitive time for them. Follow these steps to make sure that they are able to adjust properly.

1. When you get home, take the fish out of the cooler and place them in the room where you will be setting up the aquarium. This will help adjust the temperature of their bodies to the room first, as well as help them adjust from the dark environment of the cooler to the light in your room.

2. DO NOT turn on your lighting fixture yet. This may stress out the fish even more. Turn it on about a week later.

3. If a heater or chiller is required for your fish, make sure that it is already installed and that the water stabilized into the ideal temperature.

4. Take the bags of fish and have them float on top of the aquarium. Do this to adjust the temperature of the fish to the temperature of the aquarium.

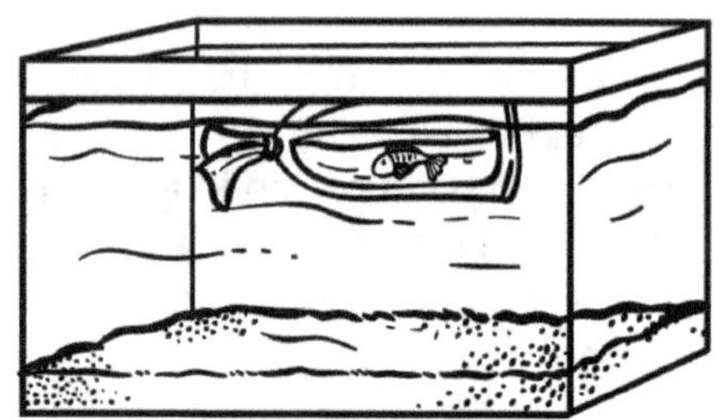

6. After one (1) hour, take the fish net and carefully net the fish into the aquarium. Throw away the plastic bag and the water in it.

7. DO NOT FEED your fish for at least twelve hours after introducing them into their new home. They are usually very nauseous at first and will tend to vomit out anything they eat, if they are in the mood to eat at all.

Your fish should be swimming around, but they probably wouldn't be as active as when you saw them at the pet store. This is normal. They will be back to normal in just 2-3 days.

If any fish unfortunately die within the next few days, remove them immediately and check for any illnesses in the remaining fish as indicated in "Step #6: Treat Sick Fish" starting on page 43.

Adding Fish to an Established Aquarium

There are times when you have already established a healthy aquarium and you want to add more fish. This can be done and many of the steps are practically the same. However, if you buy a new fish, make sure to quarantine them first.

Quarantine is a method by which you isolate a fish first to make sure it does not have any disease which could spread to your other fishes. Many aquarists lose patience in this crucial step in adding new fish. In many cases, the new fish transmits a deadly disease which kills all of the fish in the main tank.

To quarantine, do the following:

1. Buy a smaller aquarium tank or even just a plastic tub where the fish can fit.
2. Set up a filtration system for the smaller tank or tub. Place this in the same area as the main tank to ensure they have the same temperature.
3. When you acquire new fish, put them into this tank instead of your main one first.
4. After 5 days, if the fish develops no illnesses, net it and place into the main tank. If it does develop illnesses, treat the fish as in "Step #6: Treat Sick Fish" starting on page 43.

Quarantine ensures that the fish has a healthy enough immune system to kill any illnesses it might be carrying.

If you did everything in this step correctly, you should have in your possession a fully functioning aquarium with fish inside. Congratulations!

Step #5
Feed and Maintain Your Fish Properly

Feeding Your Fish

Now that you have a working aquarium with fish inside, you of course need to feed your fish. When it comes to feeding, there are many options available. Among these options, a good rule to follow is to always buy the best quality you can get. Besides, there isn't a big difference in how much you'd be spending between high and low quality fish food since a single purchase typically lasts a long time.

Good quality fish food has a nutrition label on the back of its container. This shows that the manufacturer of the fish food is honest about their product. This should show percentages (%) of protein, fats and fiber. It should also indicate that it has some vitamins and minerals like phosphorus and ash. (No, not the dust-like kind of ash. This is calcium among other things.)

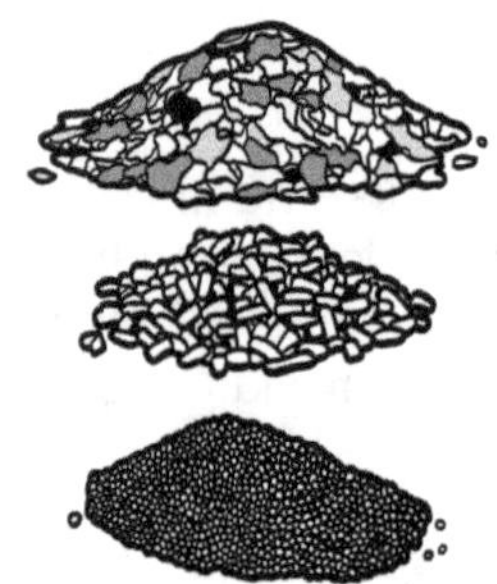

Formulated Fish Food - This usually comes in flakes, pellets or bits. While the type is not the most important thing, the nutrient content should be considered. As a beginner, it is best to simply buy formulated fish food that is suited to your fish. Some examples include flake food specific for guppies, pellets for goldfish and bits for discus. You will often find the picture of your fish or its relatives on the label of a formulated fish food container.

Freeze-dried Fish Food - This food is made by freezing the fresh food at first, preserving its nutrients and then drying it so it can be stored for a long time. It's best to occasionally add these as part of their diet instead of making it their main diet since the nutrition it contains isn't as balanced as formulated fish food. By adding these types of food, your fish are fed nutritionally more diverse food, and prevents them from becoming picky. It's like a "treat" for them as well. Some examples of this type of food include cubes of tubifex worms and spirulina (a type of nutritious seaweed).

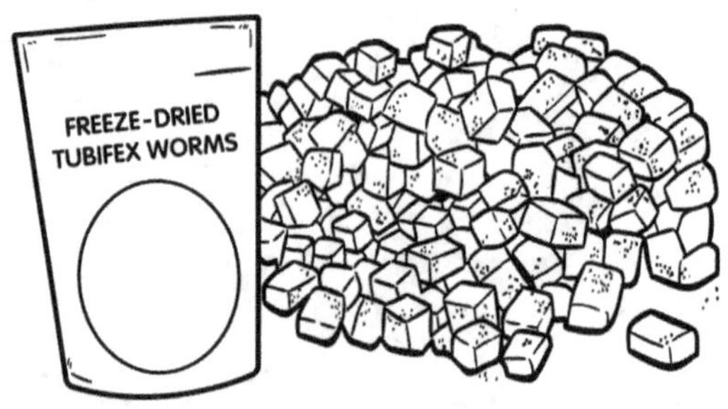

Frozen Fish Food - Aquarium fish really love this. It's nutritionally more sound than freeze-dried food, but it does take more effort to use it for feeding. To feed frozen fish food, you first need to break out a small piece then thaw it out completely by leaving it in room temperature. DO NOT feed it frozen as it will cause issues with your fish's digestive system. It also makes your aquarium dirtier than other types of food since some of it gets dissolved in the aquarium tank. Some examples of frozen fish food include beef heart mix, bloodworms, and even pieces of squid and shrimp you can mince yourself from the grocery market.

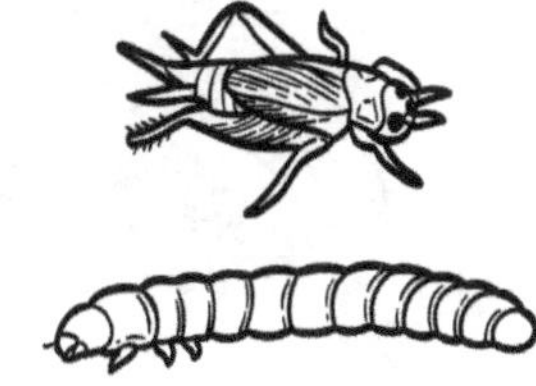

Live Food - These are usually readily available in your pet store. It's not something you give to all kinds of fish. These are reserved for certain types of fish, especially those that are predators or live on insects in the wild like the arowana. Some live food include feeder goldfish, feeder shrimp, superworms (the larva of a certain beetle) and crickets. Since they are alive, you'll need a separate container or tank for them. Many aquarists love to buy a large amount of these at a time, so it's also necessary to feed them. The simpler way to keep live food is to just buy around one week's worth of them at a time.

How to Feed Your Fish

During the first two weeks, do not overfeed your fish as this can overload your tank. Just feed them once a day. Feeding certain fish twice can help them grow bigger, but since your tank's helpful bacteria is not stable enough yet, refrain from feeding twice a day at first. Count to 30 seconds. If they finish the food within that time, that's the right amount of food you feed them. After these two weeks, you can feed your fish twice a day.

What to feed fish is often surprisingly small for some owners. For instance, for five (5) guppies in a 2.5 gallon tank, you only feed something that is smaller than a pinch.

The Problem of Overfeeding

WARNING: Just because your fish still seem hungry and they want more, it does not mean that you should feed them more. Most fish still behave in an "always look for food" attitude. This is because in the wild, food is usually scarce. When your fish are bloated, that means you've overfed them. Many fish will continue to feed themselves until they are bloated and even beyond this. They will poop almost immediately after eating and even vomit some of their food. When this happens, your aquarium will be dirtier at a much faster rate. For certain species of fish such as goldfish, this is one of the most common mistakes aquarists make that suddenly kill their fish.

<u>**Know Where Your Fish Like To Feed**</u>

There are certain types of fish that like feeding near the surface, the middle and the bottom of the aquarium. While most fish do well feeding from all areas in the aquarium, some fish, especially the ones that stay near the surface and bottom, need a type of fish food that sinks slowly or sinks quickly. Arowanas tend to be surface feeders and thus, the slow-sinking superworm is ideal. Corydoras and loaches tend to be bottom feeders and so quick-sinking pellets would be best for them.

<u>**Maintaining Your Aquarium**</u>

Other than feeding, there are a few other things you must do to maintain your aquarium. These are:

ONCE A DAY
You only need to do these tasks for a few seconds per day.

- ☑ Feed fish once or twice
- ☑ Check fish for any illnesses and if the equipment are working properly
- ☑ Keep light on during the day for display but turn it off at night (to prevent unnecessary algae growth and help fish relax at night)

ONCE A WEEK

Initially, doing these tasks will take you 20 minutes. When you get used to it, these will take less than 10 minutes to accomplish.

- ☑ Change 15-20% of the water. To do this, use the aquarium vacuum hose to displace water while at the same time, cleaning the gravel of any feces and uneaten food. Gently replace with anti-chlorine treated water so as not to bother the fish or dirty the gravel.
- ☑ Wipe any growing algae on the sides of your tank using a magnetic aquarium cleaner or a clean towel that has not been exposed to detergent.
- ☑ Take your foam filter media and wash it with running water and squeeze it. Do this whole thing again and then place it back.

ONCE A MONTH

This might involve a trip to the pet store, then just a few seconds of effort.

- ☑ Change the foam in your filter media.
- ☑ Change your biological filter media if it seems to be too icky already. You'll know it's too icky when there's a brown sludge covering your filter media.

TRIVIA! Algae is a type of microscopic plant that grows in bunches and appears like a green smudge on the sides of your aquarium glass. While a little algae isn't bad for your fish, it does make the aquarium look dirty. Make sure to clean it once a week. When you're getting too much algae, you may have overstocked your aquarium, overfed your fish or exposed the aquarium to too much sunlight.

Step #6
Treat Sick Fish

For the vast majority of pets, when a pet gets sick, the wisest thing to do would be to bring them to a vet. Unfortunately, vets that specialize in aquarium fish are not so common. Therefore, it is part of an aquarist's skill to treat sick fish. 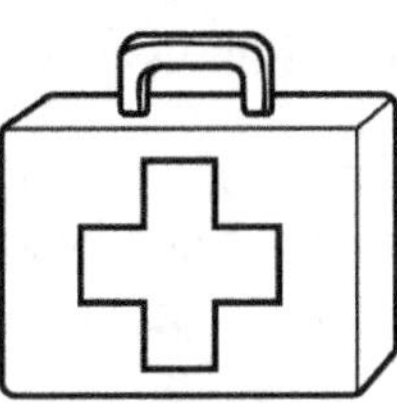

If you find a vet that you can call and visit in your area, then that would be best. This particular step is especially made for those who do not have a vet in their area.

What makes a fish sick?

Poor water quality. For most cases, a sick fish is caused by poor water quality. This happens when the water has not been changed in a long time, when fish in the water are overcrowded or when they are overfed.

Poor water quality lowers the immune system of your fish. This causes bacteria, fungi, parasites and viruses in the water to attack the fish and then make them sick.

You may need to check your ammonia levels now, to make sure it's not "off" by a lot. If your ammonia levels are high, it means you're not maintaining your aquarium properly.

As the saying goes, "prevention is better than cure." Therefore, make sure you maintain your aquarium to optimum water quality in order to avoid this problem.

Another Sick Fish. A sick fish might also be infected by another fish that was already sick to begin with. This is most common when a new fish is introduced into the tank. This is the reason why it's important to quarantine new fish. (Read more on Step #4 on page 36.)

Sometimes, a fish can be perfectly healthy one day and then just suddenly become sick for no apparent reason. This can happen even if you did everything right and maintained the aquarium properly.

Some signs that your fish is sick:

1. **White spots and/or patches** The white spots are called "ich" while the patches are called fungal infections. These usually occur due to poor water quality.

2. **Elevated scales** - This is a disease called "dropsy" and is usually a sign of a kidney infection.

3. **Visible parasites** - If you see little "strings" attached to your fish, these are probably anchor worms, small parasitic worms that attach to fish and just hang on. Aside from the treatment options found in this chapter, you need to remove them gently using tweezers.

4. **Oversized gills** - This is either a symptom of an infestation of mites, small organisms that attach and feed on fish's gills, or flukes, which are tiny parasites that infect your fish.

5. **Heavy breathing with slow, sluggish swimming** - These can mean a number of issues like an incoming sickness on other parts of this list, a wound somewhere or a sign that your fish is already at the end of its lifespan.

6. **Rubbing against objects in the aquarium** - This can mean flukes, which is accompanied by mucus on

the skin. In some cases, this can indicate the presence of fish lice, which are similar to dog ticks except smaller. Fish lice make your fish itchy which is why they rub themselves on other objects.

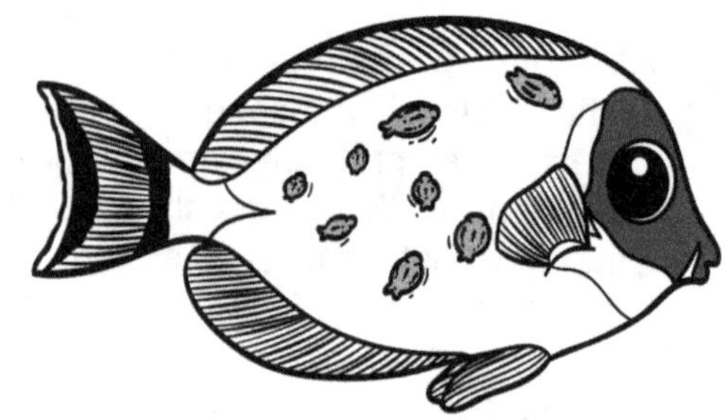

7. **Ragged, smaller fins** - This is probably due to an illness called "fin rot." However, you also need to observe because it might be due to its tank mates "bullying" one fish by biting on its fins.

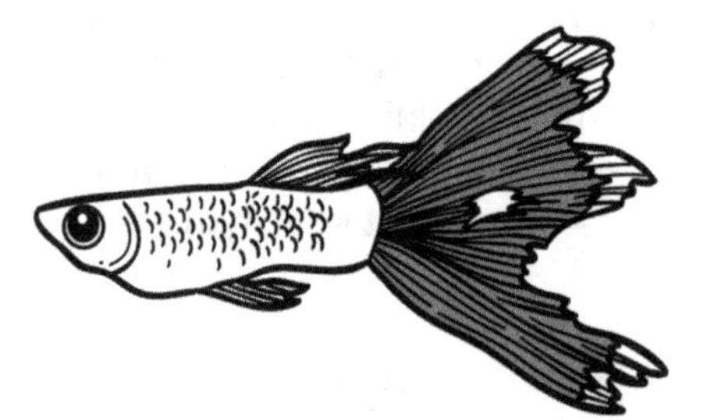

What to Do When Your Fish is Sick

As mentioned, the best option is to see a vet. However, it is also possible to simply go to a reputable aquarium store and buy the medicine that you need.

Before going to said aquarium store, take pictures of your fish and then have them on your phone or print them out. Then, look at the list of symptoms in the previous section and see which one applies most to your fish. Upon arriving at the store, show the pictures to the shop owner and tell them what you think the illness is.

The shop owner will likely recommend certain types of medication. Make sure as well that you buy medication that is from a reputable brand. One of the ways you can be sure of this is that the instructions on how the medication should be used are on the label of the medication itself.

There are a few general things to keep in mind though when applying medication:

1. Follow everything as indicated in the aquarium medication instructions when applying medication.
2. Use a quarantine tank. If you don't have one yet, buy and set one up when your fish gets sick (Read more on Step #4 on page 36)
3. You might need to use some aquarium salt as well. Replace the water of your aquarium entirely and clean everything as if setting up a new tank.
4. Remove activated carbon as a filter medium while the water has medication in it.

Dealing with the Death of Your Fish

The truth is that every aquarist, especially those who do it for a long time, will experience the death of some of their fish. This is a sad occasion that is a pain to bear for any pet keeper.

Before death, a fish will usually start breathing heavily at first. It stays at the bottom of the tank or it turns over and then starts breathing slowly. When this happens, there is usually little you can do to save it. Thus, it is advised that you move this fish to a quarantine tank and let it have its peace alone. At this point, you can only savor the last moments with your fish.

It is only right to pay respects to a fish that has already passed. Bury it somewhere outside or, if you live in a small apartment or condominium, underneath a potted plant. Invite other members of your household to share a moment with you and your departed fish.

After all, it was a member of the family as any pet is, too. It brought joy and taught you so much. Thus, a solemn moment would be appropriate and would teach a sense of healthy stewardship for all life.

Aquascaping means to arrange and add plants to your tank, as well as other things such as rocks and driftwood to make it look beautiful. It is a skill that requires a lot of practice and experience to master. This is because, just like fish, there are many aquatic plants to choose from and each require their own guide.

As for decorations, you can be as creative as you want to. You can add a wide variety of decor to your tank given that these will be safe for your fish.

In this step, some basic plants as well as the basics of aquascaping and decorating will be covered.

There are also other reasons to aquascape and decorate aside from making your tank look nice. These include:

- Providing an environment close to nature that would make some fish feel more secure

- Providing fish with hiding places when they feel shy or want to rest

- Helping keep the aquarium clean by using plants as they assist with the tank's biological process

<u>**Basic Aquascape Arrangement**</u>

Aquarist who do aquascape usually follow a rule of adding tall plants on the very back of the tank, followed by medium-sized plants in the middle and short-growing plants at the front.

Example:

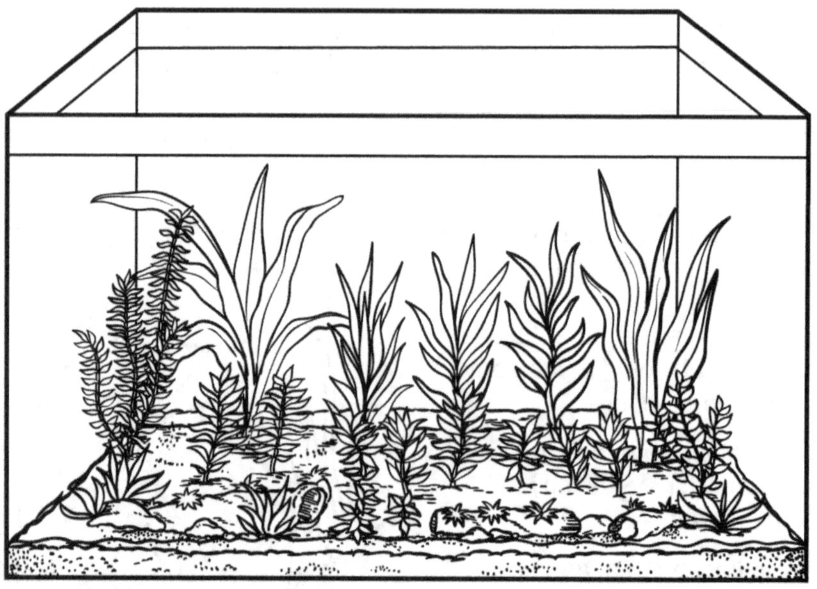

This makes sure that everything that you wish to present is visible to the viewer. This same arrangement goes for the rocks, driftwood and other decor you might want to add.

Adding Plants

Aquarium plants can be conveniently bought from the same places where you can buy aquarium fish. While there are many plants that you can add to your aquarium, some of them require more specialized care such as adding nutrients to the tank. The plants listed here, however, are very easy to keep provided that you use your usual aquarium light bulb to light it up at least 10 hours a day.

ⓐ **Java Moss** *(Taxiphyllum barbieri)* - This is a small tropical plant that is easy to keep but tends to spread fast! Each of its ends on every plant has an end part called a rhizome, which means that instead of burying its roots in the gravel, it attaches itself to something. Thus, you need to tie this to a rough rock or driftwood with ordinary thread. In about 3 months, it would be fully attached to the object you tied it to and so you can remove the thread at this point. (See page 68)

ⓑ **Anubias** *(Anubias barteri)* - This is a very beautiful, heart-shaped plant that, like the Java Moss, also has a rhizome. It looks amazing when attached to driftwood as well. (See page 68)

ⓒ **Amazon Sword Plant** *(Echinodorus amazonicus)* - This has leaves that are narrow and look like "swords." It requires its roots to be buried in gravel. To do this, first buy a 1- to 2-inch hydroponics net pot (that can be bought at any gardening store). Then, use ordinary thread to tie the roots of the plant to it. Afterwards, just bury the entire pot into the gravel. (See page 69)

ⓓ **Java Fern *(Microsorum pteropus)*** - They look like the kind of ferns you'd expect to find in a potted plant at home, only underwater. This plant is also quite easy to take care of. To plant it, do the same steps as that of the Amazon Sword Plant. (See page 69)

ⓔ **Cabomba *(Cabomba caroliniana)*** - Species of this aquarium plant come in bright green and even purple! For this reason, many aquarists want to keep it. While they are not hard to keep, they do pose a few challenges. First, that the stems are quite sensitive; so, tie and bury their stems gently into your gravel. Secondly, their leaves are like small strings that tend to float around the aquarium at first. Lastly, they grow quite tall and thus it is ideal for larger tanks. (See page 69)

TIP! Watch out for snails! Before placing your plants in the aquarium, make sure to examine it for snails. If you ever spot one, get rid of them by picking them out one by one as they can eat your aquarium plants.

Alternatively, you could also use artificial plants. Make sure you buy from aquarium stores to ensure that these plastic plants are specifically for aquarium use. This makes sure that there are no harmful substances in it such as toxic ink that could mix in the water and harm your fish.

<u>**Other Decor for Your Aquarium**</u>

Ceramic Pots - Ordinary ceramic pots make great hiding places for your fish. Simply wash them and add them to the aquarium. In many cases, they are even used by certain fish, such as cichlids, to breed!

Driftwood - Driftwood is a type of wood that has been dead for some time and has washed ashore and then treated and collected for aquarium use. It sinks to the bottom and gives the aquarium a "natural" feel. If you wish to attach a plant to it, make sure you use a rough one as their rhizomes might have a hard time attaching to driftwood with a smooth surface.

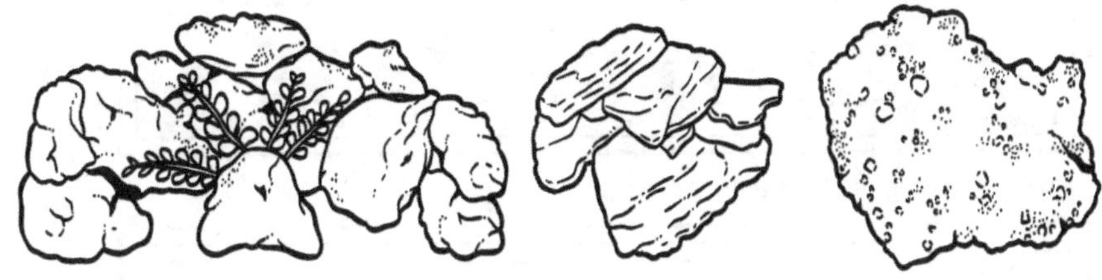

Rocks - There are different types of rocks to use for aquaria. For freshwater aquaria, you can use volcanic lava rocks, basalt and shale safely. Avoid the use of limestone as it could greatly increase your water's pH level and stress out your fish. For saltwater aquaria, you can use live marine rock. Like plants, there are artificial rocks for aquarium use which are also safe.

Glass - The use of glass bottles, beads and the like are also safe for aquarium use. These can make your aquarium look artificial instead of natural, but if done correctly, can still be pleasing to the eye. For example, orange and red beads can really complement the color of your goldfish while blue and green ones complement cichlids.

Some examples of creative set ups:

1. Aquarium with 3 layers of plants

2. Aquarium with rocks and clay pots

3. Aquarium with glass beads and bottles

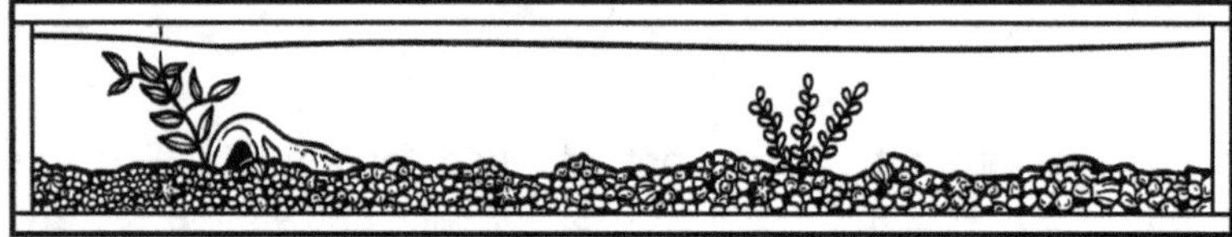

With a little creativity and imagination, you can make your tank as beautiful, unique and fulfilling as you wish. With that said, move on forward and look at some choices that you have for your aquarium!

PART 2
Fish Gallery

① Siamese Fighting Fish

② Dwarf Gourami

③ Fantail Guppy

④ Neon Tetra

⑤ Cardinal Tetra

⑥ Zebra Danio

⑦ Sterba's corydoras

⑧ Swordtail

⑨ Ryukin

⑩ Oranda

⑪ Ranchu

⑫ Green Terror

⑬ Convict

⑭ Blood-red Jewel

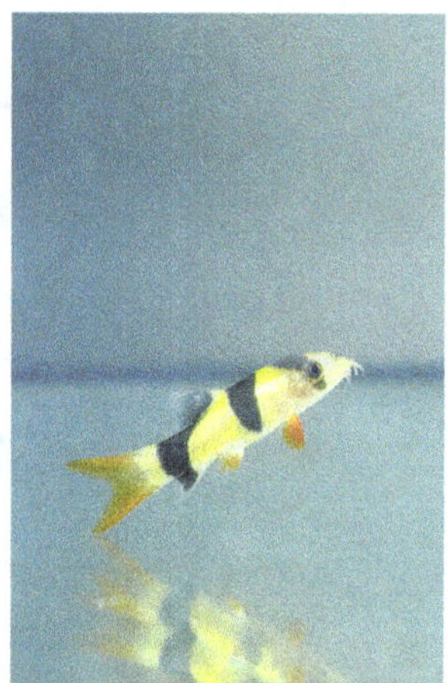

⑮ Common Pleco

⑯ Clown Loach

⑰ Freshwater Angelfish

⑱ Discus

19 Black Ghost Knife Fish

20 Pearl Gourami

21 Kissing Gourami

22 Giant Gourami

㉓ Oscar

㉔ Flowerhorn

(25) Asian Arowana

(26) Silver Arowana

(27) Common Clownfish

(28) Blue Tang

(29) Pajama Cardinalfish

(30) Coral Beauty Angelfish

(31) Peacock Lionfish

(a) Java Moss

(b) Anubias

© Amazon Sword Plant

ⓓ Java Fern

ⓔ Cabomba

Fish Gallery

In the previous pages are some fish choices you can have. There are also some aquarium plants that are mentioned in pages 51-52. This list however, is quite small compared to the huge selection that you can have as an aquarist.

They are divided into beginner, intermediate and expert and this is mostly dependent on size. However, size does not always determine how easy it is to keep a certain fish.

For example, the Electric Catfish *(Malapterurus electricus)* is only a medium-sized fish, but should never be taken care of by non-adult and inexperienced aquarists as it poses a danger via electric shock. Some very small fish can be very sensitive as well to water quality. However, the fish listed in this book don't have extremely specialized care. This makes it so that size is what separates them from one difficulty into the next.

Included in the expert section as well is a portion on marine (saltwater) aquaria. Understandably, many young readers of this book will want to jump into taking care of this type of aquarium especially since the very popular Common Clownfish *(Amphiprion ocellaris)* is on the cover of this book. However, it is highly advised that you get some experience with freshwater aquaria first before jumping into marine aquaria.

<u>**How to Use the Fish Gallery**</u>

While the general set-up and maintenance for these fish is the same, each fish can vary slightly in care as well. This is covered for each fish species when added to the 7 Steps already discussed. The information is organized for each fish in the following way:

Name *(scientific name)*
Standard length: Not to be confused with total length, this only measures from the mouth to the caudal peduncle.
Food: Suggests food items to give the fish.
Temperature: Suggests the ideal aquarium temperature that the subject fish can thrive in. For many of the species here, the temperature "24°C" is indicated for tropical temperature, with some exceptions.
Lifespan: Tells how long a fish tends to live in captivity.
Can Mix with: Suggests the type of fish the subject fish can live with in an aquarium. This is because two species that are not compatible risks them getting stressed and may even prevent them from growing properly and even cause death. In addition, always keep this rule in mind: "If it can fit in another's mouth, don't mix them together."
Description: This includes some other interesting and useful information about the fish.

<u>**Beginner Fish**</u>

These fish are small. A small tank between 2.5-10 gallons is ideal for them. This makes the aquarium inexpensive and easy to maintain and therefore good for beginners.

While these are good for beginners, they are nevertheless beautiful & amazing fish that would catch the attention of anyone looking at them.

① **Siamese Fighting Fish *(Betta splendens)***
Standard Length: approx. 1.2 inches
Food: fish flakes and freeze-dried tubifex worms
Temperature: 24°C
Lifespan: approx. 3-5 years
Can mix with: For males, other types of fish of the same size or slightly bigger than it, but not much smaller. Males CANNOT mix with other male fighting fish. For females, it can mix with same-size fishes and other females. Males are usually kept alone.
Description: This fish is unique as it is the only one in this book that can be kept without a filtration system. This is because it grabs oxygen from the air by gulping it from the surface of the water. This is why it is also normally kept in little containers or even glasses. Because of this, they are among the most popular "bring it home today" type of fish. When keeping this fish, make sure you only have one (1) male per tank as they are territorial and will fight each other, even to death.

② **Dwarf Gourami** *(Trichogaster lalius)*
Standard Length: approx. 2 inches
Food: fish flakes
Temperature: 24°C
Lifespan: approx. 4 years
Can mix with: other Dwarf Gouramis. It can live harmoniously with one (1) male Siamese Fighting Fish in the tank as well
Description: The Gourami is a relative of the Siamese Fighting Fish in that it also has the same organ that allows it to gulp air from the surface of the water. However, Gouramis do not do this to the same extent as the Siamese Fighting Fish which is why they have to be kept in a fish tank with a working filtration system. Males are gorgeous with their metallic blue and red tiger stripes while females have a nice shine to them.

③ **Fantail Guppy** *(Poecilia reticulata)*
Standard Length: approx. 0.7 inches (males); approx. 1.2 inches (females)
Food: fish flakes
Temperature: 24°C
Lifespan: approx. 2 years
Can mix with: other similarly sized and peaceful fish like swordtails and tetras
Description: The fantail guppy belongs to the livebearer family. They are called "livebearers" because, unlike most fish that lay eggs, they give birth to live young. The fantail guppy is probably the most recognizable small fish in aquaria and one of the most attractive as well because of the many colors they can have. They tend to dazzle with their mixture of orange, blue, and dark green colors.

④ **Neon Tetra** *(Paracheirodon innesi)*
Standard Length: approx. 0.6 inches
Food: fish flakes
Temperature: 24°C
Lifespan: approx. 8 years
Can mix with: other similarly sized and peaceful fish like guppies and tetras
Description: The Neon Tetra is one of the most iconic fish to the aquarist. Its shiny, neon blue stripe and red belly tends to look amazing with a planted aquarium. It's also easier to keep and smaller than its cousin, the Cardinal Tetra. It is a fish that feels comfortable in a school, so keep at least five (5) fish if you're going to keep the Neon Tetra.

TRIVIA! You call a group of lions a pride, wolves a pack and birds a flock. For fish, a group is called a school. Not all fish, however, are schooling fish. Some prefer to be alone and just socialize with others of its kind during breeding.

⑤ **Cardinal Tetra** *(Paracheirodon axelrodi)*
Standard Length: approx. 1 inch
Food: fish flakes
Temperature: 24°C
Lifespan: approx. 5 years
Can mix with: other similarly sized and peaceful fish like guppies and tetras
Description: The Cardinal Tetra is the bigger and a little bit more sensitive cousin of the Neon Tetra. Many more experienced aquarists tend to favor this species over its cousin because the striking color is more visible on a bigger fish. It is, however, more expensive and more prone to getting sick if not maintained properly. Keep at least five (5) specimens as it schools like its cousin.

⑥ **Zebra Danio** *(Danio rerio)*
Standard Length: approx. 1.5 inches
Food: fish flakes
Temperature: 24°C
Lifespan: approx. 3 years
Can mix with: other similarly sized and peaceful fish like guppies and tetras
Description: The Zebra Danio, is one of the iconic beginner's fishes for a number of reasons. First, it has a striking coloration of black and off-yellow that earned the "zebra" in the name. Secondly, they are an active fish that is just fun to watch. Lastly, of course, they are easy to keep. They are also a schooling fish and need to be kept in groups of five (5) or more.

⑦ **Sterba's Corydoras** *(Corydoras sterbai)*
Standard Length: approx. 2 inches
Food: sinking pellet food
Temperature: 24°C
Lifespan: approx. 5 years
Can mix with: other similarly sized and peaceful fish like guppies and tetras
Description: Corydoras refers to a large group of related miniature catfishes. Like many catfishes, they tend to be bottom feeders. Thus, they look especially nice when put together with other small fish that tend to dwell the top and middle portions of the tank like guppies and tetras. You can buy almost any corydoras and its care wouldn't be very different from this one. They are also a schooling fish and thus need at least three (3) of them in one tank.

⑧ **Swordtail** *(Xiphophorus hellerii)*
Standard Length: approx. 2 inches (males); approx. 2.5 inches (females)
Food: fish flakes
Temperature: 24°C
Lifespan: approx. 3 years
Can mix with: other similarly sized and peaceful fish like guppies and tetras
Description: It's like a bigger version of the guppy, though less colorful. The males have a striking "sword" extension to their caudal fin. Females simply look like bigger guppies.

TRIVIA! For many species of fish so far, the male is more beautifully colored and adorned than the female. While it's not completely clear with some species, it is thought that the males use this to attract potential mates just like some birds like peafowls do.

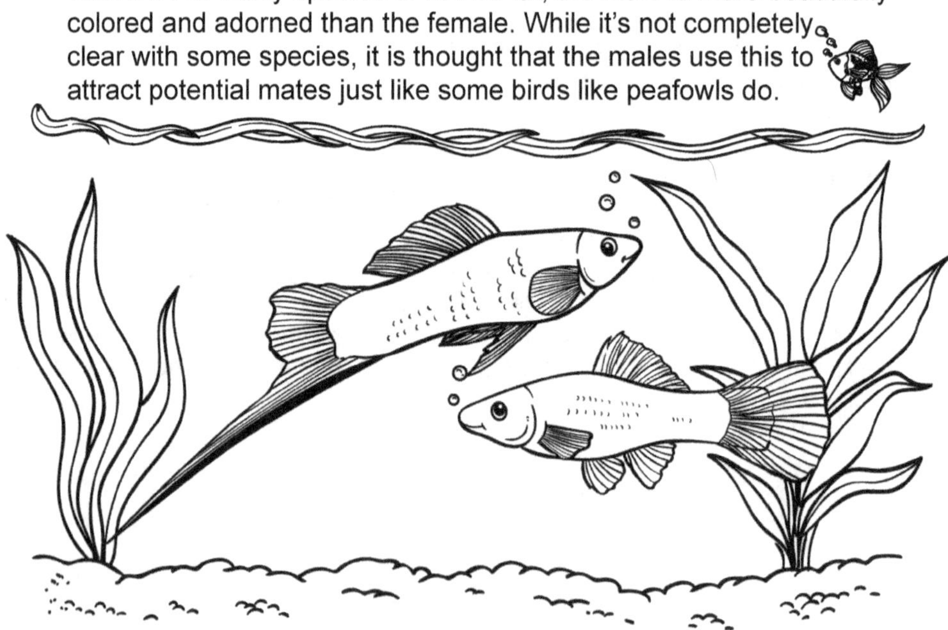

<u>**Intermediate Fish**</u>

When you want to move into the 15- to 45-gallon range, you get the chance to keep some of the most coveted kinds of aquarium fish. In this range, you have aquarists who specialize in keeping only a certain type of fish such as Discus and Goldfish. Who knows, maybe you'll also be a fan of a specific type of fish here.

Goldfish *(Carassius auratus)*

When one mentions the word "aquarium," the first fish people imagine would probably be the goldfish. The goldfish is a coldwater fish, meaning that it thrives in colder than tropical temperatures in the wild. However, captive bred ones have adjusted to the usual tropical temperature used by most aquaria.

The goldfish has won the hearts of many aquarists due to its cuteness, coloration and relatively simple care. In China, it has been selectively bred around a thousand years to create many variations in terms of size, color and body characteristics. Today, many countries continue to do this with goldfish. There are even goldfish-exclusive shows where the most beautiful goldfish win awards much in the same manner as dog shows! In this book, three of the medium-sized goldfish will be discussed.

One minor difference in caring for goldfish is in feeding. This is due to their digestive system being very simple as compared to other types of fish. Feed your goldfish 2-3 very small feedings instead of one big one. Do not give them big feedings as this could kill them. Overfeeding is one of the most common mistakes of beginner goldfish aquarists.

⑨ **Ryukin** *(Carassius auratus)*
Standard Length: 5 inches
Food: specialty pellets for fancy goldfish
Temperature: 24°C
Lifespan: 5-10 years
Can mix with: other Ryukins
Description: Of the three, the Ryukin is the easiest one to take care of. It's not so sensitive to water conditions. However, it is a little aggressive so it's best to place them with other Ryukins.

⑩ **Oranda** *(Carassius auratus)*
Standard Length: 5 inches
Food: specialty pellets for fancy goldfish
Temperature: 24°C
Lifespan: 5-10 years
Can mix with: other Orandas
Description: The Oranda is also simple to take care of, but can be a bit more fragile than the Ryukin. They have beautiful wavy fins that are prone to being attacked by other fish, so it's best to just keep it with other Orandas. Be strict with yourself with weekly water changes.

⑪ **Ranchu** *(Carassius auratus)*
Standard Length: 5 inches
Food: specialty pellets for fancy goldfish
Temperature: 24°C
Lifespan: 5-10 years
Can mix with: other Ranchus
Description: The Ranchu is sometimes called the "King of Goldfish" in Japan. This is because it looks like a little precious jewel that swims in your aquarium. Of the three examples in the book, it is the rarest and most expensive type of goldfish. Due to its unwieldy body, make sure you keep the water flow at a minimum in the aquarium.

<u>**Medium Cichlids**</u>

Cichlids are among the most diverse fish kept in aquaria. They come from all over the world and range in a wide variety of colors, sizes and temperaments.

The cichlids contained in this book is a small fraction to what's available out there. For typical cichlids, they tend to be simple in their care but tend to be aggressive as well. Therefore, they need to be kept with others that can fend for themselves. They are also very intelligent and they usually know who their owners are. For this bunch of unique traits, cichlids are dubbed by aquarists as "fish with attitude."

For medium-sized cichlids, three are described as follows:

⑫ **Green Terror** *(Andinoacara rivulatus)*
Standard Length: approx. 8 inches
Food: formulated cichlid pellets, frozen bloodworms
Temperature: 24°C
Lifespan: approx.10 years
Can mix with: other cichlids like it that can fend for themselves or low-activity fish such as the plecostomus
Description: The striking color is what makes this fish a great keep and beautiful to behold. The combination of metallic green and blue combined with its fins lined bright orange gets better with age if fed and taken care of properly. It can also benefit from feeding on frozen bloodworms to improve its color. As its name suggests and like other cichlids, it can be quite aggressive. Males have a slight hump which shows up when they grow bigger.

⑬ **Convict** *(Cryptoheros nigrofasciatus)*
Standard length: approx. 6 inches for males; approx. 5 inches for females
Food: formulated cichlid pellets
Temperature: 24°C
Lifespan: approx.10 years
Can mix with: other cichlids like it that can fend for themselves or low activity fish such as the plecostomus
Description: This is one of the easiest cichlids to keep and is highly recommended for first time cichlid keepers. For this species, males are larger and have black stripes on their gray body. Females are smaller and have orange patches all over. Remember, it is still a typical cichlid and can get aggressive at times.

⑭ **Blood-red Jewel** *(Hemichromis lifalili)*
Standard length: approx. 3 inches
Food: formulated cichlid pellets, frozen bloodworms
Temperature: 24°C
Lifespan: approx.10 years
Can mix with: other cichlids like it that can fend for themselves or low-activity fish such as the plecostomus
Description: This is also one of the easier cichlids to keep, but with much benefit. It has a blood-red body with brilliant blue shiny spots. While it is one of the smaller cichlids, it is also quite aggressive like others of its kind. So much so that it can hold its own even with fish a little larger than itself like the convict.

<u>**Bottom-Dwellers**</u>

Like the Corydoras, these medium-sized fish are ideal to have if you want fish that dwell at the bottom of your tank.

⑮ **Common Pleco *(Hypostomus plecostomus)***
Standard length: approx. 10 inches
Food: Plant-based pellets that sink, algae that grows inside your tank
Temperature: 24°C
Lifespan: approx.10-12 years
Can mix with: other cichlids that can fend for themselves. It fights with other plecostomus so keep only one (1) per tank.
Description: This vegetarian catfish is one of the easiest fish to keep. It is sometimes called the "janitor fish" because it cleans algae from the side of tanks, and is also one of the reasons why aquarists like adding it. It typically stays hidden for most of the day and then comes out at night to feed. Since it keeps to itself most of the time, it's a good companion for many other types of fish like goldfish and cichlids.

⑯ **Clown Loach *(Chromobotia macracanthus)***
Standard length: approx. 6 inches
Food: pellet-based food that sinks; frozen bloodworms
Temperature: 24°C
Lifespan: approx. 20 years
Can mix with: cichlids, but note that cichlids grow much faster than they do. Otherwise, other peaceful fish would suffice.
Description: The appearance of the Clown Loach is very striking. Its orange body with dark black stripes makes it one of the most popular aquarium fish around. They are a schooling fish that need to be kept in groups of five (5) or more.

<u>**"Round" Cichlids**</u>

While not an "official" classification, these two cichlids are two of the most popular aquarium fish in the hobby. They both happen to not look like most other cichlids since they are round. They also do not behave like other cichlids since they tend to be quite peaceful.

⑰ **Freshwater Angelfish** *(Pterophyllum scalare)*
Standard length: approx. 3 inches
Food: flakes, bit pellets
Temperature: 24°C
Lifespan: approx. 8 years
Can mix with: other peaceful species.
Description: It is likely called an angel for its gracefulness in appearance and movement. Freshwater Angelfish are one of the most kept and bred aquarium fish. For this reason, it is one of the best beginner fish at this size. Just don't keep it with aggressive species since its fins are prone to being nipped.

⑱ **Discus** *(Symphysodon discus)*
Standard length: 5 inches
Food: specialized bits food for discus, frozen beef heart mix
Temperature: approx. at 24°-27°C, with 27°C as most ideal
Lifespan: approx.10 years
Can mix with: other peaceful species
Description: This fish is one of the most beautiful aquarium fish because it comes in many colors and patterns. It does require you to be a skilled aquarist as it requires very clean water. Keep them in groups of at least three (3) and change 15% of the water thrice a week.

<u>**Medium-Sized Gourami**</u>

These are related to the Siamese Fighting Fish and the Dwarf Gourami found in the beginner's section. Like the first two, these aren't hard to take care of and are quite interesting types of fish.

⑲ Black Ghost Knife Fish *(Apteronotus albifrons)*
Standard length: approx.15-20 inches
Food: small, slow-sinking pellet bits; frozen bloodworms
Temperature: 24°C
Lifespan: approx.10 years
Can mix with: a wide variety of fish even smaller than it is, especially when brought up with its companions. It does not tend to be aggressive although it does display this a little bit at times.
Description: It is one of the most unique aquarium fish you can ever buy. It has a smooth, jet-black body with a smoothly undulating fin on its underside. This is the largest in the medium-sized section because it is compatible with smaller fish, even cichlids and discus. It is technically blind as it looks for food using a weak electric organ. Even through its blindness, it somehow senses its owner especially after many years of interacting. It can even be trained to feed from its owner's hand as with many fish in the following section.

㉠ **Pearl Gourami** *(Trichopodus leerii)*
Standard length: approx. 4 inches
Food: flakes, pellets
Temperature: 24°C
Lifespan: approx. 4 years
Can mix with: other pearl gourami and peaceful bottom-dwellers such as the Plecostomus and the Clown Loach. It can be aggressive with other males of its species, so keep only one (1) male with other females.
Description: This is an easy fish to keep with beautiful coloration. It gets its name from the many spots it has that shine like pearls. Males have a slight red patch near their belly and are, just like previous gourami shown, more brilliantly colored than the females.

㉑ **Kissing Gourami** *(Helostoma temminckii)*
Standard length: approx. 8 inches
Food: flakes, pellets
Temperature: 24°C
Lifespan: approx. 7 years
Can mix with: other Kissing Gourami in a group of 5-10
Description: This fish is best kept as a group because the males tend to have displays of strength between them that look like kissing. More than their appearance, it is this interesting and adorable display that makes them ideal for a species tank. To see the kissing effect, keep a group of them in one tank.

TRIVIA! A species aquarium is fish tank that only contains one type of fish. This highlights any particular behavior the fish tend to like in a community such as that of the Kissing Gourami or when Discus like to face a single direction together.

Expert Fish

These fish require a bigger tank in the 50-, 75-, 100-gallon range or even bigger. This is due to their size or that they need a more stable water chemistry that a bigger tank can give. Since they are in bigger tanks, they take more effort to maintain or require specialized care. The fish here tend to be more expensive than the fish previously mentioned, with a few exceptions. When you move to this spot, you are basically saying that you're ready to be a very serious aquarist!

The freshwater fish mentioned in this chapter are usually displayed in a bare tank. This means that there's no gravel and only a filter is used. This makes the tank easier to clean, making sure that an aquarium vacuum hose is able to get all of the waste and uneaten food. But more than that, it allows the regal view of these large fish to stand out. Because of their size, no background is necessary in order to impress their audience!

㉒ **Giant Gourami** *(Osphronemus goramy)*
Standard length: approx.16 inches
Food: large fish pellets
Temperature: 24°C
Lifespan: approx. 20 years
Can mix with: as young fish, can be kept with other Giant Gourami and other fish of the same size. However, as medium-sized and fully grown fish, it tends to be aggressive towards fish it did not grow up with.
Description: The Giant Gourami is a majestic looking fish that's never absent in freshwater fish exhibits. While caring for it is simple, it tends to eat a lot which also messes up an aquarium faster. Though it only grows up to 16 inches, a 75- to 100-gallon minimum capacity is required for it since it makes a huge mess. Like many large species, it can get very personable with its owner, often celebrating its owner's arrival (maybe excited to be fed) and allowing it to be stroked.

Large Cichlids

These cichlids are large enough that they require an aquarium reaching up to a 50-gallon capacity and above. For the two fish mentioned here, it's actually ideal to have one fish per 50 gallons so that each fish can reach their maximum size and thereby achieve their majestic look.

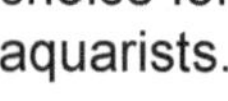 **Oscar *(Astronotus ocellatus)***
Standard length: approx. 15 inches
Food: large fish pellets
Temperature: 24°C
Lifespan: approx.10 years
Can mix with: other Oscars of the same size. Otherwise, keep them alone.
Description: Despite the fact that the Oscar isn't really a beginner's fish due to its size and aggressive nature, many people still keep it because of how simple it is to take care of. It is not very sensitive to water changes. Perhaps, the greatest draw to the Oscar is its personality. It is a fish that knows its owner, allows itself to be stroked and can even be moody at times. This means that there will be days when an Oscar is extremely happy to see you and times when they shrug you off and try to ignore you. When it comes to keeping large aquaria, Oscars seem to be the first choice for freshwater aquarists.

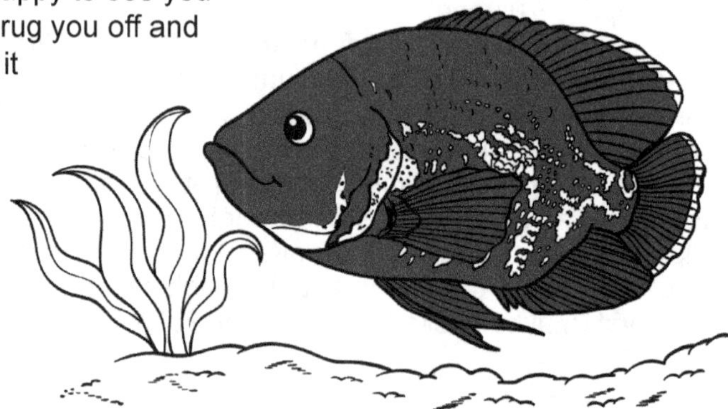

㉔ Flowerhorn

Standard length: approx. 10 inches for males, approx. 8 inches for females
Food: specially formulated Flowerhorn food
Temperature: 24°C
Lifespan: approx.10 years
Can mix with: no other fish. Keep it alone.

Description: If you haven't already noticed, the Flowerhorn does not contain a scientific name. The reason for this is that the Flowerhorn is not a fish found in nature but a hybrid between several types of cichlid. The result is an aggressive, magenta-colored, large fish that has won the hearts of many aquarists in recent years. It typically has varying color patches that change with age, but the shade of magenta on it is what is attention-grabbing. During adulthood, it also develops a large hump on its head that catches even more attention. Like goldfish and discus, it now has contests all on its own and people compete for the best-looking Flowerhorn.

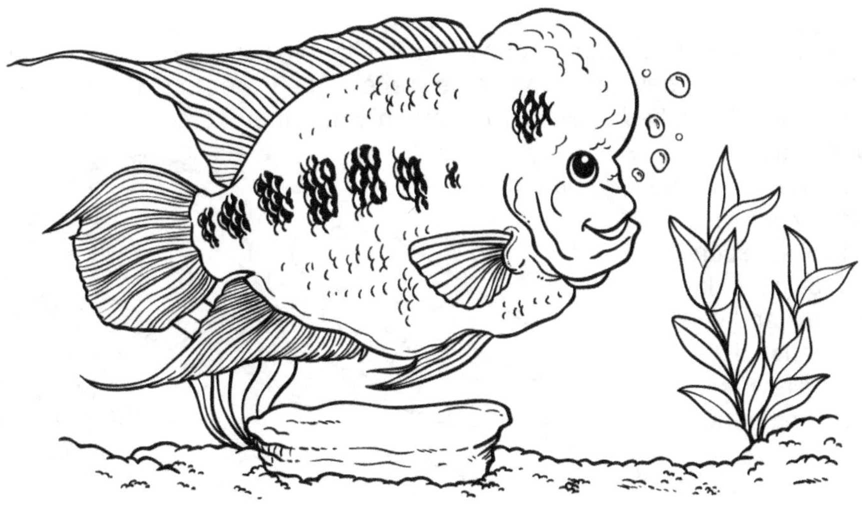

Arowana

If there were an iconic "big" fish in the aquarium, it would be the Arowana. It is called "Dragon fish" in Chinese aquarist tradition. There are many species of Arowana worldwide.The ones featured in this book include the common ones sold in local pet stores and are thus not so expensive. However, many of these fish can command very expensive price tags, especially the Asian red varieties. Some even go higher than the ₱1,000,000 mark!

Taking care of an Arowana is relatively simple, though since it requires such a big tank, it's a little challenging to maintain. For starters, many aquarists mistake its feeding habits for exclusively eating live food. Actually, it's best to feed it floating pellets as it swims near the surface most of the time. With this said, it's good to feed it live food every once in a while. It's best kept alone in a bare tank because it looks amazing on its own as a fully grown fish. As a young fish, it can be kept in 35- to 50-gallon tanks but will need to move to 100- to 200-gallon tanks as it matures.

The most common mistake that people make with this fish is not securing the lid of the tank. In the wild, they jump from the surface of the water to catch insects. Thus, many aquarists have had their hearts broken when they come home to find their Arowana dead
on the floor, after it tried to jump out.
In summary, feed it
appropriately, secure the
lid and provide a big
enough tank and you'll
be an aquarist of
one of the crown
jewels of the hobby.

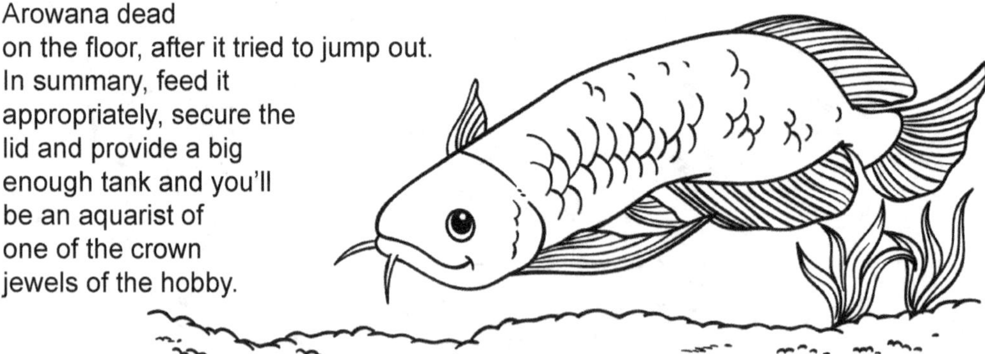

㉕ Asian Arowana *(Scleropages Formosus)*
Standard length: approx. 36 inches (when fully grown)
Food: floating pellets specifically formulated for Arowanas, live insects like crickets and mealworms
Temperature: 24°C
Lifespan: approx. 10 - 20 years
Can mix with: other arowanas and similarly large fish but only in aquaria in the 400 gallon and above range. For this reason, it is normally kept alone in the home aquarium.
Description: The Asian Arowana is found in various color varieties, usually depending on the location of their parents in the wild and their breeder. Green, gold and various shades of red and orange are the typical colors you'd find. This type of arowana as well has a wide price point – ranging from the price comparable to buying movie tickets for two people to buying a car!

㉖ Silver Arowana *(Osteoglossum bicirrhosum)*
Standard length: approx. 36-48 inches (when fully grown)
Food: floating pellets specifically formulated for Arowanas, live insects like crickets and mealworms
Temperature: 24°C
Lifespan: approx. 10 years
Can mix with: other arowanas and similarly large fish but only in aquaria in the 400-gallon and above range. For this reason, it is normally kept alone in the home aquarium.
Description: Especially when grown up, it is flattened from the side and looks sleek with its silver-bluish shiny scales with just a tint of green. The Silver Arowana is a good species to start with. For one, it is readily available and inexpensive. Another reason is that virtually all of the specimens are bred in captivity. This means that Silver Arowana sold in pet stores are used to being kept in an aquarium already.

<u>**The Marine Aquarium**</u>

A saltwater aquarium is called a marine aquarium. The fish you can keep in a freshwater tank differ from a saltwater tank. The colors of many saltwater fish also tend to be more attention-grabbing than that of freshwater fish. For this reason, many aquarists prefer to keep this type of aquarium.

While it is much harder, keeping a marine aquarium is well worth the effort. You'll need to know the basics covered in all the steps, along with a few more things to have and do to keep a marine aquarium. These things are:

1. While you can easily keep very small freshwater tanks, the minimum size for a beginner's marine aquarium is 45 gallons. While there are exceptions, smaller marine tanks are actually harder to maintain as their ammonia, pH and salinity levels (the salt content of the water) tend to be more unstable as well.

2. You need to monitor ammonia (the levels of toxicity as a result of fish waste), pH (whether it's kept between 7.6 - 8.4) and salinity levels and keep them at ideal levels.

3. You need to cycle your aquarium before putting fish inside. Unlike most freshwater aquarium fishes, you can't buy your marine fish and set up your aquarium on the same day. In order to do this, you need to set up your marine aquarium and then add a liquid culture of helpful bacteria. From this point, you need to let it just run with the filter on for 1 month. You then check ammonia, pH and salinity levels to see if they are adequate. After this, you can add fish inside the aquarium.

4. You need to note these additional equipment for marine aquaria:

Protein Skimmer - This device is connected to a second aquarium pump and it helps maintain proper ammonia levels. Over time, these show up as a foamy substance that goes inside the cup above your tank.

Hydrometer - This measures salinity, or the amount of salt in your aquarium. This device floats on top of the water in your tank and when the water hits the green area, it means that the salinity levels in your tank are proper.

Liquid Bacteria Culture - This comes in a small bottle that you can buy from aquarium stores and then add to your saltwater aquarium. This is important in helping your aquarium cycle first. To learn more about the concept of cycling, go back to page 90.

pH and Ammonia testers - While these are also used for freshwater aquaria, these are essential for marine aquaria. The pH of marine aquaria need to be kept between 7.6 - 8.4. The right ammonia level for marine aquaria is usually indicated in the testing kit that you buy.

Live Rock and Marine Substrate While a regular gravel substrate is good for freshwater tanks, marine tanks require live rock and some sort of marine substrate such as white beach sand. This is related to the pH level you need to maintain. The addition of live rock and white beach sand tends to increase the pH and helps stabilize it. Live rock also contains helpful bacteria that would be useful in cycling your aquarium later on.

Aquarium Salt - You need to buy aquarium salt to mix in with the water. Do not use ordinary salt you buy from the store but salt specifically for marine aquarium use. Mix the right amount of salt (as per the instructions) after you add the substrate in. Measure with a hydrometer and make sure it's stable at that level for about a month before adding fish.

<u>**Tropical Fishes for a Marine Aquarium**</u>

㉗ Common Clownfish *(Amphiprion ocellaris)*
Standard length: approx. 3 inches
Food: formulated fish food for Clownfish or marine aquarium fish
Temperature: 25°C
Lifespan: approx. 5 years
Can mix with: other peaceful, similarly sized fish and perhaps its corresponding Bubble-tip Anemone *(Entacmea quadricolor)*
Description: This is one of the easiest marine aquarium fish to keep. They are not too sensitive to water conditions and typically stay in place, especially when you keep it with its corresponding anemone.

㉘ Blue Tang *(Paracanthurus hepatus)*
Standard length: approx. 10 inches
Food: marine aquarium formulated fish food, plant-based food like spirulina
Temperature: 25°C
Lifespan: approx.10 years
Can mix with: other Blue Tangs as it is a schooling fish.
Description: This fish is challenging to keep since it is a schooling fish. To keep them, you'd be looking at a minimum of five members for a 75-gallon tank! However, they are fun and beautiful to look at in such a set-up since they actively swim all day.

TRIVIA! For some reason, people try to mix the Clownfish and the Blue Tang together. However, because they have such drastically different needs, it isn't a good idea to put them in a single aquarium.

㉙ **Pajama Cardinalfish *(Sphaeramia nematoptera)***
Standard length: approx. 3 inches
Food: marine aquarium formulated fish food
Temperature: 25°C
Lifespan: approx. 5 years
Can mix with: other peaceful tank mates
Description: The Pajama Cardinalfish looks unique from snout to tip. It has an interesting mix of colors including red, black and yellow with a pattern of fish unlike any other. Like the Clownfish and the Coral Beauty Angelfish, this is an easy saltwater fish to keep. It's a schooling fish, which means you'll have to keep at least 5 or more in a tank.

㉚ **Coral Beauty Angelfish *(Centropyge bispinosa)***
Standard length: approx. 3.5 inches
Food: marine aquarium formulated fish food, spirulina
Temperature: 25°C
Lifespan: approx. 5 years
Can mix with: other non-aggressive fishes
Description: Saltwater Angelfishes are very different from their freshwater counterparts. In the marine aquarium, they tend to be easy to take care of and stunning in appearance. However, most of them tend to be quite large—growing into the 8- to 12-inch range. The Coral Beauty is different in this regard and is considered a "dwarf" angelfish. It is a solitary species and, while it may tolerate other tank mates, do not place it with fishes of the same species or appearance to it.

③① **Peacock Lionfish (*Pterois volitans*)**
Standard length: approx. 12 inches
Food: Live food, but can be trained to eat thawed frozen shrimp pieces
Temperature: 25°C
Lifespan: approx. 10-15 years
Can mix with: peaceful tank mates that are bigger than it
Description: Lionfishes are voracious predators that can swallow fish instantly with its large mouth. For this reason, you should never keep it with fish smaller than it. There are several species of Lionfish available, but this is the most common. At first, you'll probably need to feed it live feeder fish and shrimp, but it can be trained to take frozen shrimp after some time of wiggling the food in its face with tweezers. To keep it comfortable, also place it in an aquarium with live rock as it uses coral reefs for camouflage. Watching it hunt is certainly entertaining —
staying completely still until a fish comes near it. When its prey is within gulping distance, the feeding is so fast it looks like it just opened its mouth and its prey just vanished!

<u>**Start off with Fish of Mind**</u>

If you have read every word and gone back and forth reading various parts of the book, you should be ready to start your own aquarium.

Don't worry about it when things get a little confusing at first. Over time, things will be smooth and easy for you even at the expert level.

Realize as well that this book only contains very few types of fish you can take care of. When you visit your local aquarium store, you'll encounter more types of fish of various colors, shapes, features and difficulty in terms of maintenance. Ask that aquarium store as well as do your own research on the Internet to find out how to care for these other types of fish.

Remember that the best teacher in aquarium keeping is experience. Get more experience, learn from your mistakes and develop your instinct. As mentioned in the beginning of the book, doing this for years will eventually lead to you developing your own style as an aquarist.

Whether it be a small 2.5-gallon aquarium with a few guppies or eventually marine aquaria that can accommodate even larger marine creatures, remember to always have respect for life and be good stewards of your pets. Treat them with respect and they will bring you reward and fulfillment.

Good job on you for starting on this journey! May this book not only develop your skill as an aquarist, but your character as a person.

PART 3
Frequently Asked Questions (FAQs)

Frequently Asked Questions (FAQs)

These are some questions beginner aquarist may have as they gain more experience. Often, these are answered via research but a few important topics are covered here.

Q If I make an aquarium with a lot of filters, does that mean I don't have to change water as often?

A Yes, you can put a lot of filters, but it will never compensate for regular water changes. The discipline of weekly water changes is far more effective in maintaining clean water. Besides, not all types of dirt are removed by the filter, and so a few water changes here and there never really hurt.

Q I saw some very beautifully planted aquaria on the internet as well as at some aquarium stores. How do I set this up?

A If you want to fill your tank with plants, note that the species and the number of plants you put also makes them more difficult to keep. Sometimes, you'll need carbon dioxide supplements and more intense, full-spectrum lighting for certain plants. It's best to study the specific care of certain plants and then find out if these plants are indeed compatible.

Q My aquarium store sells other kinds of animals aside from fish that can be kept in an aquarium. Can I keep them with my other fish?

A It depends, but if you're a beginner, I wouldn't recommend it. But if you wish to try, don't forget to follow the rule of thumb that "if one fits in another's mouth, don't put them together!" This doesn't solve all the issues, so here are some specific rules depending on what you're going to put with your fish:

• **Turtles** - Most freshwater turtles sold as pets such as the Red-eared Slider *(Trachemys scripta elegans)* are semiaquatic, meaning that they spend some time on land and some time in the water. So you need to set up a space where they can go on land and back into the water. There are also truly aquatic turtles such as the Pig-nosed Turtle *(Carettochelys insculpta)* that spend all their time in the water, and can be kept in an aquarium with fish the same size as it.

However, an added complication with turtles is that they need natural sunlight and/or a specialized UV bulb to help them grow and survive. Thus, I generally wouldn't recommend putting them with your fish.

• **Salamanders, Newts and Axolotls** - These are lizard-like amphibians that are close relatives of frogs. Just like many turtles, salamanders and newts are semiaquatic and need land to climb on. Axolotls are fully aquatic and can be kept with certain fish. The main issue with these amphibians is that they need to be kept at temperatures way lower than most tropical fish and may need an aquarium chiller and a thermometer. Thus, take extra care in buying them and bringing them home.

• **Lobsters, Shrimps and Crabs** - When done right, these shellfish can thrive easily with aquarium fish as most species sold in aquarium stores are scavenger types that
 don't grow very large. This means that they like cleaning out the aquaria of dirt on the bottom and can add a very interesting vibe to your aquarium.

Q I want to breed my fish. How do I do this?

A In the beginning of this book, it was mentioned that, compared to other pets, aquarium keeping is easier for the most part. However, it's the other way around when it comes to breeding fish.

For many other pets like mammals and birds, the parents of the pet take a very active role in rearing the newborn. For fish, most of them do not take care of their fry (baby fish) and even those that do only do so until a certain extent.

Baby fish are also born extremely tiny—usually resembling tadpoles the size of a dot made by a ballpoint pen. This makes feeding very difficult and maintaining optimum conditions in the aquarium much harder since the babies are very sensitive. However, it is not impossible to do, but it is highly suggested that you become more comfortable with taking care of fish first for at least a year or so before attempting to breed.

When you think you are ready, do more research on how to breed your specific fish as there are different methods for different types of fish. Remember as well that not every fish can easily be bred in captivity. A good beginner fish to breed would be the Siamese Fighting Fish *(Betta splendens)* as well as the various livebearers like guppies and swordtails.

Q I heard that there is such a thing as the "brackish water aquarium." I heard it was a cool set-up. What is this?

A Brackish water refers to the mixture of fresh and saltwater. In the wild, these would be areas called estuaries, where rivers and the ocean meet. It has a unique ecosystem where you have mangrove trees and species specific to brackish water. The most notable fish in brackish water systems are the Archer Fish and the Mudskipper. The Archer Fish shoots down insects by spitting water from the surface. Mudskippers "skip" on land and are therefore called "walking fish."

Treat the brackish water aquarium as a saltwater aquarium. Monitor its salinity levels closely and use aquarium salt. In addition, you can "half-fill" an aquarium to include areas for branches for Archer Fish to shoot down feeder crickets and land areas for Mudskippers to skip on. Sounds tough? Well yes, the brackish water aquarium is quite an advanced type of tank. However, as with anything in this hobby, put in the work and it will reward you well.

Q I read this book, and then I looked at stuff on the Internet/other books and found some information in this book contradictory to what these sources say. What do I believe?

A Early in the book, it was mentioned that the hope was for you to develop your own style. As different aquarists, it is very likely that the experience of the two aquarists may contradict. The best advice is to try both out and see what works for you. If it works for you, it honestly doesn't matter if it doesn't work for 100 other aquarists. You will eventually develop your own style.

Q What is the author's favorite aquarium fish?

A The TOP 5 are most definitely:

1. Black Ghost Knife Fish - because of its jet-black appearance and affection for its owner
2. Discus - because of their colorfulness, challenge in breeding and since they require work
3. Clownfish - because they are active and easy to keep
4. Green Terror - because it just looks great due to the combination of orange, green and blue which doesn't occur very often
5. Neon Tetra - because they look pretty

Bibliography

Scott, Peter W. (1995). "The Complete Aquarium". New York: DK Publishing, Inc.

Mills, Dick (2002). "You & Your Aquarium". Canada: Alfred A. Knopf.

Christian, Matthew. (2000). "Aquarium Style". New York: Barron's.

Acknowledgments

To my my parents Allan and Elnor for allowing me to use my allowance to keep all sorts of pets growing up — especially aquarium fish and supporting me to odd ends.

To my siblings Boyet, Franz and Francis for supporting me as my partners in petkeeping even when I tended to overdo it.

To my Uncle Fritz who generously gave his 50-gallon aquarium to his then adolescent but forever grateful nephew.

To the Catabijan family and the whole community of Saint Matthew's Publishing Corporation and Kahel Press — thank you for believing and trusting in me. How you've treated me is far more than what I deserve for sure.

To the Philippine community of aquarists who shared their valuable time and knowledge with me since I was a kid. I want to especially thank one of the best breeders in the country—Michael Go for allowing the Kahel Press Team to take pictures of his amazing and beautiful fish and even checking the manuscript for this book.

To my wife Julz and my daughter, Jordyn, for being the best reasons to get up every morning and do what I need to do.

Most of all, to Jesus who saved me by His grace and allowed me the freedom to express myself freely such as in the endeavor in writing this.

Thank you.

About the Author

Fiel John Meria is a man who is happily married to Julz. As of this book's writing, he is about to be a dad in just a few months.

He started to keep aquaria at about the age of 9 and has never quite stopped. He also kept and bred other animals including hedgehogs and rabbits.

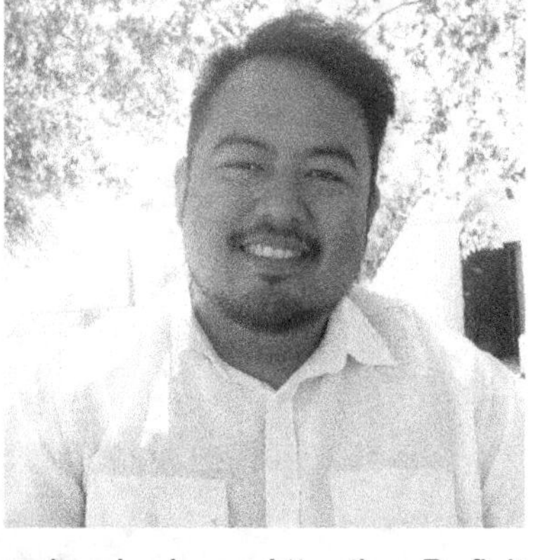

He is the Director of PROJECT POND (Project People Overcoming Neurodevelopmental Difficulties) where he life coaches and travels with people who have Attention-Deficit Hyperactivity Disorder, Autism Spectrum Disorder and Specific Learning Disabilities. He and his wife are both diagnosed with ADHD and dedicate themselves to sharing the love of Jesus to families who have children and members with special needs.

kahel press Children's Books

Purchase copies online!

www.stmatthews.ph

www.ingramcontent.com/pod-product-compliance
Lightning Source LLC
Chambersburg PA
CBHW081256130726
47998CB00010B/2819